Lacy Little Knits

Lacy Little Knits

BEAUTIFUL DESIGNS & INTRIGUING TECHNIQUES

IRIS SCHREIER

LARK CRAFTS

An Imprint of Sterling Publishing Co., Inc.
New York

WWW.LARKCRAFTS.COM

Editor:
LINDA KOPP

Art Director:
DANA IRWIN

Cover Designer:
MEAGAN SHIRLEN

Technical Consultant:
ELLEN LIBERLES

Fashion Consultant/Stylist:
R. BROOKE PRIDDY

Assistant Editor:
SUSAN KIEFFER

Associate Art Director:
LANCE WILLE

Art Production Assistant:
JEFF HAMILTON

Editorial Assistance:
MARK BLOOM

Illustrator:
ORRIN LUNDGREN

Cover Photographer:
MEAGAN SHIRLEN

Photographer:
JOHN WIDMAN

The Library of Congress has cataloged the hardcover edition as follows:

Schreier, Iris.
  Lacy little knits: clingy, soft, & a little risque / Iris Schreier.
      p. cm.
  Includes index.
  ISBN 1-57990-717-2 (hardcover)
  1. Knitting--Patterns. I. Title.
   TT825.S3925 2007
   746.43'2041--dc22

                                        2006036752

10 9 8 7 6 5 4 3 2 1

Published by Lark Crafts
An Imprint of Sterling Publishing Co., Inc.
387 Park Avenue South, New York, NY 10016

First Paperback Edition 2011
Text © 2007, Iris Schreier
Photography and illustrations © 2007, Lark Crafts, an Imprint of Sterling Publishing Co., Inc.

Distributed in Canada by Sterling Publishing,
c/o Canadian Manda Group, 165 Dufferin Street
Toronto, Ontario, Canada M6K 3H6

Distributed in the United Kingdom by GMC Distribution Services,
Castle Place, 166 High Street, Lewes, East Sussex, England BN7 1XU

Distributed in Australia by Capricorn Link (Australia) Pty Ltd.,
P.O. Box 704, Windsor, NSW 2756 Australia

The written instructions, photographs, designs, patterns, and projects in this volume are intended for the personal use of the reader and may be reproduced for that purpose only. Any other use, especially commercial use, is forbidden under law without written permission of the copyright holder.

Every effort has been made to ensure that all the information in this book is accurate. However, due to differing conditions, tools, and individual skills, the publisher cannot be responsible for any injuries, losses, and other damages that may result from the use of the information in this book.

If you have questions or comments about this book, please contact:
Lark Crafts
67 Broadway
Asheville, NC 28801
828-253-0467

Manufactured in China

ISBN 13: 978-1-57990-717-4 (hardcover) 978-1-4547-0138-5 (paperback)

For information about custom editions, special sales, premium and corporate purchases, please contact Sterling Special Sales Department at 800-805-5489 or specialsales@sterlingpub.com.

For information about desk and examination copies available to college and university professors, requests must be submitted to academic@larkbooks.com. Our complete policy can be found at www.larkcrafts.com.

CONTENTS

INTRODUCTION

How can something as beautiful as knitted lace be so frustrating? And knowing that, why on earth do we feel so strongly compelled to create it? Is it the challenge—the knitting world's equivalent to Mt Everest? Maybe it's the satisfaction one feels upon creating breathtakingly intricate designs. Does it require a bottomless pool of patience, eagle eyes, an infinite amount of spare time and devoted concentration? I've tossed out the rules and developed techniques that do away with charts and patterns that must be followed line by line. Instead I've learned—and I'll teach you —how to look at the knitted fabric and intuitively understand how to build the next row. I call this technique "reading your lace," and it's wonderfully liberating. No longer a slave to the pattern, you're free to take your project on the road, to start and stop on a whim, and even knit while watching TV. And the results are utterly feminine, and not the least bit fussy. Airy, lacy, and sometimes clingy, these flirty little knits are made for double takes. Let the yarn do some of the work. Add some angles to make the lace pattern look more elaborate and advanced.

Here you'll find a collection of patterns that most knitters would have fun knitting regardless of their level of expertise. Beginners will find patterns that provide a new spin on very simple lace motifs. Simple techniques such as alternating yarns and incorporating elongated stitches and two-stitch repeats create lovely knitted pieces. Some of the stitches actually look like they're floating in air. More experienced knitters will appreciate those patterns that are completely unique in construction, varying from top down, to bottom up, to center out for symmetry. And some unique knitted stitches will bear an uncanny resemblance to crochet.

In a continuation of my previous books, *Exquisite Little Knits* (co-authored with Laurie Kimmelstiel) and *Modular Knits*, my goal is to help you think differently about your knitting. In this book I have included some projects that are probably unlike anything you have knitted previously. If you've done any modular knitting, you know that knitting on angles can be a lot of fun, particularly when you're working with multiple colors or variegated yarn. It's a whole new experience when coupled with lace. Suddenly, the lace ridges run in opposite directions, intrigue builds, as does the excitement, and the knitting becomes positively addictive and difficult to stop.

Besides being fun these techniques give you the ability to create incredibly figure-flattering shapes. Garments knitted on the diagonal are visually trimming because they direct the eye upward, resulting in a slimmer, proportion-pleasing look. For example, I have sized the Perfect Choice Sweater (page 130) up to size 2X because this piece will flatter any figure.

Thumb your way through the chapters and you'll see that the first two include projects that are fairly standard, but build in difficulty until, before you know it, you're constructing lovely garments by adding knitting to sheer fabric, or shaping a piece by knitting side to side with a simple slip stitch. Here also you'll be introduced to techniques for letting yarns like mohair, cashmere, and silk ribbon add lightness, transparency, and drape to your knitted pieces.

The last three chapters include multidirectional projects that take that type of knitting to new levels of visual interest. From the simple Chevron Ruana (page 96) with its slimming "v's" to the more advanced Celestial Tie Wrap Jacket (page 138), I've designed garments that highlight just how versatile continuous modular techniques can be.

Select from a wide variety of tops, tanks, and wraps. For those knitters who want to be adorned in knitwear from head to toe, there's a romantic matching flared skirt and tee set (complete with elegant lace insets) and even a trendy self-belted sheath dress. Make them in your favorite colors and prepare for the compliments to come.

Ready to create unique garments with hassle-free lace designs? Just pick your favorite projects and follow the instructions. Be sure to read through the Basics chapter to get a sense of how the stitch patterns work and how to read your lace. I urge you to pursue this type of knitting...you won't regret it. And for sure, you'll never be bored!

BASICS

There are a variety of patterns in this book ranging from very easy to more advanced designs. Some use common stitches; others require more complex and unusual ones. Some pieces have little or no shaping, while others are shaped and formed with lace.

My goal is for you to be able to understand the construction of the garment you're knitting to the point of being able to knit it without having to follow line-by-line instructions. This makes the knitting more fun and even addictive.

That's why I recommend that, regardless of what level knitter you are, you read through this section, paying particular attention to the information on stitch patterns and following your lace.

STITCH PATTERNS

LONG STITCH AND DOUBLE LONG STITCH

This is usually a double long stitch. It is formed over 2 rows. In this book elongated stitches are used as decorative elements to enhance and open the knitted fabric.

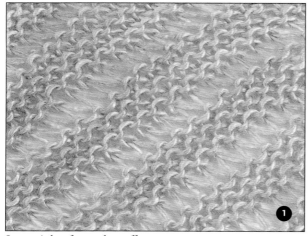

Long stitches form a lacy effect.

Directions: Insert the needle into the next stitch as though to knit. Normally, you would wrap the working yarn around the needle one time in order to pull a new stitch from the old stitch, and after pulling the loop through you would drop the old stitch from the needle. To create the elongated stitch, wrap the working yarn twice (instead of the usual one time) around the needle, and draw both loops through to form two stitches on the right needle. After you have pulled the double loop through, drop the old stitch from the needle. On the return row, only knit into the first loop of the double wrap, dropping the second loop to form a long stitch.

In some projects you'll be instructed to make a Double Long stitch; this is formed by wrapping the yarn around the needle three times when knitting. On the return row, only knit into the first loop of the triple wrap.

OPENWORK STITCH

This is an easy 2-stitch pattern that is used extensively in this book. This stitch forms the openings or eyelets in the knitting to·make the lace pattern.

Directions: First row: *yo, SKP; repeat from * to end. Usually a knit stitch is added at the beginning and end of each row.

Following row: Always slip the previous row's SKP stitch and knit the previous row's yo stitch.

Following your lace is important for you to keep track of any inadvertently dropped or missing yo stitches—a very common mistake. This will maintain a consistent and even fabric.

TRAVELING LACE

A major theme in this book is to read your knitting. This is the most important thing you can learn to do as you work on projects. It will free you from having to carry around and refer to cumbersome patterns and charts, and will

Lacy Little Knits

Lining up lace pattern.

allow you to concentrate on your piece and how it is constructed. You will catch errors before you have taken them too far, and prevent much frustration.

It may not look like it, but creating the lace in this book is really quite simple—the eyelets and lace ridges patterns being clear to follow. Two projects that will require you to "read" your lace and follow the pattern are Diagonals in Flight (page 84), and the Floating Stitch Tank (page 52). In Diagonals in Flight for example, you will notice that the eyelets (openings) run on the diagonal. That means that the knitting shifts over on every other row (the lace is only knitted on every other row, with the alternate rows knitted or purled across). The pattern will be spelled out in order to establish the pattern. From that point on, you will follow it in sequence by reading your lace.

It is also important to note that new lace panels start when there are enough stitches available. On the Right Front, for example, when working the right side rows, you are instructed to knit across all extra sts at the end when there are fewer than five stitches and a full lace pattern repeat cannot be completed. You will need to add a new lace panel in sequence at the beginning of the row whenever there are five knit stitches.

EXERCISE ONE

Here is a good practice exercise for learning how to follow your lace. This is helpful for some patterns in the book, such as the Floating Stitch Tank (page 52):

Lace Pattern

Row 1: ★yo, slip 2 sts together as if to knit, k1, then pass both slipped sts over k st, yo, k3; repeat from ★ to last 3 sts, yo, sl 2tog, k1, p2sso, yo.

Row 2: Purl across.

Note: Whenever there are not enough stitches to knit a complete lace stitch pattern, simply knit across those remaining stitches. Line up all lace ridges at all times.

Cast on 17 sts.

Row 1: K1, work Row 1 of Lace Pattern to last st, k1.

Row 2 and all even-numbered rows: K1, work Row 2 of Lace Pattern to last st, k1

Rows 3 through 8: Repeat Rows 1 and 2 three times more.

Row 9: K2tog, work Lace Pattern in established pattern to last st, k1—16 sts.

In other words: K2tog, k5, work Lace Pattern once (yo, sl 2tog, k1, p2sso, yo, k3), to the last 4 sts, yo, sl 2tog, k1, p2sso, yo, k1.

Row 11: K1, work Lace Pattern in established pattern to last st, k1—16 sts.

In other words: K1, k5, work Lace Pattern once (yo, sl 2tog, k1, p2sso, yo, k3), to the last 4 sts, yo, sl 2tog, k1, p2sso, yo, k1.

Row 13: Inc 1, work Lace Pattern in established pattern to last st, k1—17 sts.

In other words: Inc 1, k5, work Lace Pattern once (yo, sl 2tog, k1, p2sso, yo, k3) to last 4 sts, yo, sl 2tog, k1, p2sso, yo, k1.

Row 15: K1, work Lace Pattern in established pattern to last st, k1—17 sts.

In other words: K1, work Lace St (yo, sl 2tog, k1, p2sso, yo, k3) twice, to last 4 sts, yo, sl 2tog, k1, p2sso, yo, k1.

As you can see from this example, a decrease at the beginning of Row 9 prevented you from knitting the first Lace Pat panel, as established in Rows 1 through 8. So instead, you k5 across the 5 remaining stitches. But after Row 13, when there are once again enough stitches to reinstate the Lace Pat panel, it is knitted again. Always use the lace ridges and eyelets as a guide as to where the new row's lace panel must be inserted. And if there are not enough stitches (in this case fewer than 6), knit across them instead of working the Lace Pat.

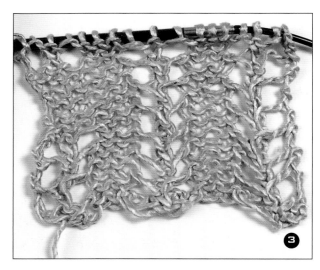

❸

On the left side one lace pattern repeat is removed when there are insufficient stitches to complete it (after a decrease at the edge)—instead the remaining stitches are knitted. The lace pattern repeat is added again when there are sufficient stitches (after an increase at the edge).

As you can see, the eyelets will line up from previous rows.

Here is a second exercise that will help you work on multidirectional traveling lace in Chapter 5:

EXERCISE TWO

Lace Pattern

Row 1: Edge stitch (as specified in pattern), ★yo, sl 1, k2tog, psso, yo, k3; repeat from ★ to last 4 sts, yo, sl 1, k2tog, psso, yo, edge stitch (as specified).

Row 2: K across.

Cast on 3 sts.

STEP 1: Build width of Center-Increase Triangle

Row 1: K1, inc 1, p1—4 sts..

Row 2: Inc 1, inc 1, k1, p1—6 sts.

Row 3: Inc 1, k1, inc 1, PM, k2, p1—8 sts.

Row 4: Inc 1, k to marker, RM, inc 1, PM, k to last st, p1—10 sts.

Row 5: Inc 1, yo, sl 1, k2tog, psso, yo, RM, inc 1, PM, yo, sl 1, k2tog, psso, yo, k1, p1—12 sts.

Row 6 and all even-numbered rows: Inc 1, k to marker, RM, inc 1, PM, k to last st, p1—2 sts increased.

Row 7 and all odd-numbered rows: Inc 1, work Lace Pat as established to marker, RM, inc 1, PM, work Lace Pat as established to last st, p1—2 sts increased.

This means that you work the even-numbered rows as for Row 6 and all odd-numbered rows as follows:

Row 7: Inc 1, k1, yo, sl 1, k2tog, psso, yo, k1, RM, inc 1, PM, k1, yo, sl 1, k2tog, psso, yo, k2, p1—16 sts.

Row 9: Inc 1, k2, yo, sl 1, k2tog, psso, yo, k2, RM, inc 1, PM, k2, yo, sl 1, k2tog, psso, yo, k3, p1—20 sts.

Row 11: Inc 1, k3, yo, sl 1, k2tog, psso, yo, k3, RM, inc 1, PM, k3, yo, sl 1, k2tog, psso, yo, k4, p1—24 sts.

Row 13: Inc 1, k4, yo, sl 1, k2tog, psso, yo, k4, RM, inc 1, PM, k4, yo, sl 1, k2tog, psso, yo, k5, p1—28 sts.

Row 15: Inc 1, k5, yo, sl 1, k2tog, psso, yo, k5, RM, inc 1, PM, k5, yo, sl 1, k2tog, psso, yo, k6, p1—32 sts.

Row 17: Inc 1, add new lace panel as follows: (yo, sl 1, k2tog, psso, yo); then, k3, continue existing lace panel: (yo, sl 1, k2tog, psso, yo); k3, add new lace panel: (yo, s1, k2tog, psso, yo); RM, inc 1, PM, add new lace panel: (yo, sl 1, k2tog, psso, yo); k3, continue existing lace panel: (yo, sl 1, k2tog, psso, yo); k3, add new lace panel: (yo, sl 1, k2tog, psso, yo); k1, p1—36 sts.

Note that because you increased twice on each row, after 12 rows you have added 24 stitches, and at this point you

Squared-off Sides with lace panels running diagonally away from the center. As you can see, they are discontinued (knitted across) when they reach the edge. But new lace panels will be added as stitches are increased in the center (top).

have enough sts to insert 4 new lace panels, 1 before and 1 after the previous lace panel on each side of the center increase, ending with a total of 6 lace panels. **Important:** Always add lace panels on both sides of the center increase on the same row for symmetry.

For example, if you were to continue working an additional 12 rows, at the end of Row 29 there would be 10 lace panels (5 on each side of center increase), with one panel added at each outer edge (beyond the previous panel) and one added on each side of the center increase. For this exercise, end the piece at Row 18: Inc 1, k16, inc 1, k16, k1, p1—38 sts.

STEP 2: Square off the sides maintaing 38sts every row

Row 1: K1, work Lace St as established to marker, RM, inc 1, PM, work Lace St as established to last 2 sts, p2tog.

Row 2: K to marker, RM, inc 1, PM, k to last 2 sts, p2tog.

Repeat Rows 1 and 2 until piece is at desired length.

In other words, to repeat these 2 rows, you will be working as follows:

Row 1: K2, (yo, sl 1, k2tog, psso, yo), k3, (yo, sl 1, k2tog, psso, yo), k3, (yo, sl 1, k2tog, psso, yo), k1, RM, inc 1, PM, k1, (yo, sl 1, k2tog, psso, yo), k3, (yo, sl 1, k2tog, psso, yo), k3, (yo, sl 1, k2tog, psso, yo), k1, p2tog—38 sts.

Row 2: K18, RM, inc 1, PM, k17, p2tog—38 sts.

Row 3: K1, (yo, sl 1, k2tog, psso, yo), k3, (yo, sl 1, k2tog, psso, yo), k3, (yo, sl 1, k2tog, psso, yo), k2, RM, inc 1, PM, k2, (yo, sl 1, k2tog, psso, yo), k3, (yo, sl 1, k2tog, psso, yo), k3, (yo, sl 1, k2tog, psso, yo), p2tog—38 sts.

Row 4: Repeat Row 2.

Row 5: K6 (you have just knitted across the previous row's lace panel because you no longer have enough stitches to maintain it—k1 needed to maintain selvage-st edge and k5 for pattern is insufficient), (yo, sl 1, k2tog, psso, yo), k3, (yo, sl 1, k2tog, psso, yo), k3, RM, inc 1, PM, k3, (yo, sl 1, k2tog, psso, yo), k3, (yo, sl 1, k2tog, psso, yo), k5, p2tog (you have now omitted the last lace panel from the previous row)—38 sts.

Row 6: Repeat Row 2.

Row 7: K5, (yo, sl 1, k2tog, psso, yo), k3, (yo, sl 1, k2tog, psso, yo), k4, RM, inc 1, PM, k4, (yo, sl 1, k2tog, psso, yo), k3, (yo, sl 1, k2tog, psso, yo), k4, p2tog—38 sts.

Row 8: Repeat Row 2

Although the stitch count remains the same once you square off the sides of the triangle, you will find that when you add lace panels they will always be at the center (on either side of the center increase); when you discontinue lace panels by knitting across them, they will always be at the edges (see row 5 on previous page). This is because you are increasing the number of stitches at the center and decreasing the number of stitches at the edge.

Important: Continue working an additional 16 rows by repeating original Rows 1 and 2. Then compare your swatch to photo 4. This will be the real test of whether you have learned follow your lace, since row-by-row instructions are not provided in this last repeat.

UNUSUAL LACE

There are several patterns in the book that use a lace technique that resembles crochet. It involves decreasing 3 or more stitches in the middle of the work to leave a single remaining stitch at the center of the group, and then adding new stitches to that center stitch. Here are some close-ups:

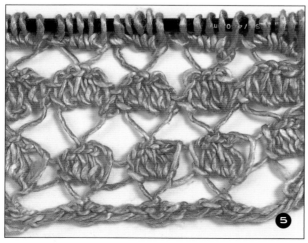

Silk swatch in progress

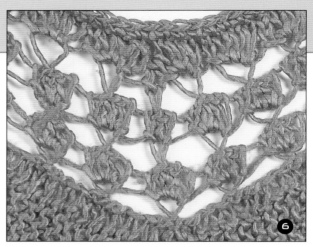

Diagonal Lace Shell

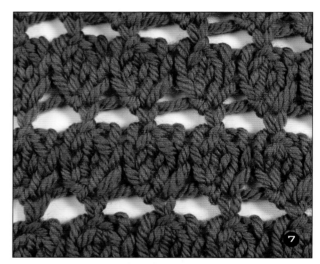

Faux Crochet Cropped Bolero

TIPS FOR SUCCESS

Some of this book's patterns are unusual in their construction. Even experienced knitters (and especially experienced knitters who are used to standard techniques) may misunderstand the instructions and become frustrated if they presuppose that they understand what to do without reading through this section. Please approach these projects with an open mind as though you are knitting these types of patterns for the first time. Following are some specific suggestions for a successful outcome.

READ YOUR WORK

It is a common mistake to assume that there is something wrong with your knitting because it does not resemble the specified shape. Please note that because the projects in chapters 3 through 5 are not conventionally knitted across, they will never look "right" on the needles. To check the shape and measurements of your piece, remove the stitches from the knitting needles as follows: Thread a tapestry needle with a length of yarn (at least 1 yd or 1 m long). Draw the threaded needle through the stitches and slide them off the knitting needle. Lay the fabric completely flat and unstretched to determine the shape and measurements.

To continue on the piece, return the stitches to the knitting needle, being careful to keep them in the proper order, with markers in place, and without twisting the stitches.

Here are some other pointers that are helpful for chapters 4 and 5 in case you drop your marker or lose your place. In order to assure success, you must learn to read your work.

Increases in the center-increase triangles (chapters 4 and 5) take place at the beginning and center of each row. You can tell which stitch requires the increase by tracking the pair of stitches from the previous row that represent the very centermost point of your row; they are closely joined because that was the position of increase in the previous row, and both loops emerged from one stitch. You can feel that by tugging on them, and if you flip your work over, you'll notice that one of the stitches is actually a ½ stitch in that it does not have any "roots" in other stitches, but hangs suspended since it was just added. This is the stitch where you'll always work the center increase.

Squaring off the sides of triangles is done in a way that balances the number of increases to the decreases in each row, so the stitch count remains the same on each row.

Squaring off the top of the center-increase triangle (or binding off) is generally done in two parts. The row is divided in half and each half is worked separately. Decrease on both ends of each half, until there are 2 or 3 stitches left. Bind off these remaining stitches. Cut yarn. Repeat on the other side, making sure to attach yarn and start knitting at the centermost point.

Leaving Unworked Stitches in the center-increase triangle creates a V neckline. This technique is used in the Diagonal Lace Shell and the Perfect Choice Sweater when the right and left sides of these pullovers are worked separately. Stitches are left behind in order to form the "V" neckline, which is later knitted in the opposite direction connecting the 2 sides (see photo 8).

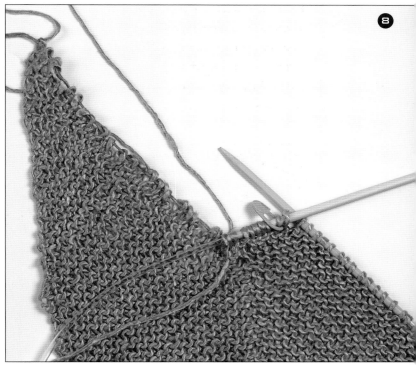

Stitches are left behind (1 stitch per ridge) while the right side is being worked to create V.

MEASURE YOUR WORK

Probably the most important thing you can do to ensure proper fit is to ensure that you are on gauge with your knitting. Here are some special tips for doing this:

If you're working with silk, note that it is a fiber with very little "give," meaning that it barely stretches or springs back when you knit. It is ideal for lace because it requires little blocking to open up the eyelets. However, knitted fabric with silk becomes very stretchy, and this additional ease must be taken into account when you swatch, measure, and knit the garments. Often, silk garments look small but fit well when worn. An example is the Soiree Skirt, which looks much smaller when knitted than when actually worn—it will stretch out for up to 12"/30.5cm around the hips, for example.

Be very careful trying to substitute rayon or cotton in fitted multidirectional garments. Check not only the gauge, but the weight of the yarn. If your yarn is heavier than the one used in the garment, the knitted fabric will weigh more and may not fit properly.

So choose your substitute yarn based on the yards/meters per ounces/grams.

There are a number of projects that start with center-increase triangles in this book (chapters 4 and 5). These projects require that your work be on flexible needles in order to see the shape forming. In addition, you will generally be instructed to measure the width of the piece at the base of the triangle.

To check the measurements of your triangle, remove the stitches from the knitting needles as follows: Thread a tapestry needle with a length of yarn (at least 1 yd or 1 m long). Draw threaded needle through the stitches and slide them off the knitting needle. Lay the fabric completely flat and unstretched to determine the measurements (see photo 9).

Measuring your work

To continue working on the piece, return the stitches to the knitting needle, being careful to keep them in the proper order, with markers in place, and without twisting the stitches.

RECOMMENDED TOOLS

Good needles can make all the difference in your knitting experience. For silk, cashmere, and mohair, Rosewood needles work especially well. Rosewood is softer than bamboo, smooth, and extremely lightweight. These needles have

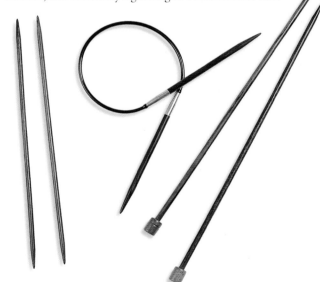

Rosewood needles—double pointed, circular, and straight versions (left to right)

become popular now and are available through most yarn shops and online re-sellers. You will find that your hands do not get tired with these needles, and the yarn stays put without slipping. Because most of the lace patterns here require yarn-over stitches, and because this type of stitch tends to get hung up on the joints of circular needles, be very careful about the circular needles that you select. Make sure to find circular needles that have smooth joins and plastic cords (like the ones on page 14) that do not fight you.

Use markers that can be easily clipped on and will stay put with a locking device, and are just as easily removed. They will give you the most flexibility in these patterns.

TECHNIQUES USED

This section includes a review of standard techniques that are used in this book. Most of the techniques described are commonly used in many knitting patterns on the market today.

PICKING UP STITCHES IN FABRIC

Many different sheer fabrics can be used in the Tulle-Trimmed Top shown on page 28. It is essential to select a fabric that does not unravel when cut, and tulle is perfect. Use a small crochet hook to punch even-sized holes in the fabric along one edge. Then with your working yarn held behind the fabric, start using the crochet hook to draw loops of yarn through the fabric and place them on your needle.

LOOSE CAST OFF METHOD AND CROCHET BIND OFF

The easiest way to cast off loosely is by using larger needles. If these are not available, merely knit every

other stitch twice before binding it off. Work as follows:

Knit one stitch. Transfer it back to the other needle. Knit it again. Bind it off by pulling the second stitch on the needle over the first on the needle.

Another method of loosely binding off is with a crochet bind off.

Insert a crochet hook through first stitch to be cast off as if you were knitting it, catch yarn on hook and draw it through the stitch on the needle (new stitch is now on crochet hook), drop original stitch from needle. Continue working as follows: ★Insert hook into next st on needle knitwise, catch yarn on hook, drawing it through the st on the needle and in one continuous motion, draw it through the previous stitch on the hook. One stitch is now bound off, the new stitch is on the hook; drop the original worked st from the needle. Repeat from ★ across until all stitches are bound off. Cut yarn and fasten off last st on crochet hook.

SHORT ROWS WITH AND WITHOUT WRAPS

Short rows are used throughout the book, and in most cases on the diagonal (in all the projects in chapters 3, 4, and 5).

Diagonal short rows require no wraps, so there is not much to say about them here, except that it is important to follow the instructions exactly and NEVER stop to take a break in the middle of a row. Always take a break only after you have knitted back and all your stitches are on one needle. Sometimes that is hard in the setup phase of knitting where there are quite a few cast-on stitches that must be worked, so make sure to dedicate a nice amount of time without a break for starting a new project.

However, Gwenivere's Choice Tunic (page 64) uses short rows that are knitted in a standard fashion. You will find that the instructions tell you to wrap and turn the short rows.

Wrap short rows as follows: If purling in the pattern, when instructions say "wrap and turn," slip the next stitch purlwise, bring the yarn between the needles from the front to the back, slip the same stitch back to the left needle, and turn the work, bringing yarn to the knit side between the needles. If knitting in the pattern, when instructions say "wrap and turn," slip the next stitch purlwise, bring the yarn between the needles from the back to the front, slip the same stitch back to the left needle, and turn the work, bringing yarn to the purl side between the needles.

Then on the way back you will pick up the wrap along with the stitch that has been wrapped in order to close up any holes. This helps to make a smooth transition between the extra row and the preceding and following ones.

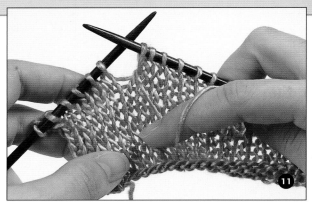

Bring yarn from back to front between both needles.

Slip wrapped stitch back to left needle.

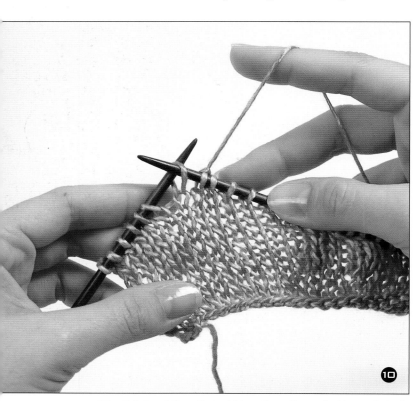

Slip stitch from left needle to right needle as if to purl with yarn in back.

When all short rows are worked, knit as usual to the wrapped stitch. Insert the needle knit wise into the wrap and the stitch that was wrapped. Then knit the wrapped stitch together with the wrap as shown in order to hide the wrap. This technique will prevent holes from forming where you turned your work.

Lacy Little Knits

Slip stitch from left needle to right needle as if to purl with yarn in front.

Slip wrapped stitch back to left needle.

Bring yarn from front to back between both needles.

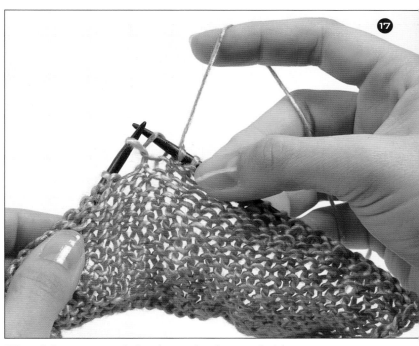

When all short rows are worked, purl as usual to the wrapped stitch. Then insert the needle from behind into the back loop of the wrap as shown and place it on the needle. Purl the wrap along with the stitch that was wrapped in order to hide the wrap. This technique will prevent holes from forming where you turned your work.

CARRYING TWO YARNS UP ALONG SIDE OF WORK

When one yarn is used for two rows:

It is fairly simple to carry one yarn up along the side when working with the other. Not much thought needs to be given when the yarns alternate every other row.

When one yarn is used for 4 rows:

When yarn is carried along for more than two rows, as in the Soho Overskirt on page 38, it becomes more difficult and requires some attention.

To work the Soho Overskirt, for example, you will need to fasten the unworked yarn every 2 rows by twisting it from behind and around to the front of the working yarn. Otherwise the loopy edge will be unattractive and detract from the garment. Make sure not to pull too tightly or leave the yarn too loose; you will need to maintain good tension so that the piece will lie properly.

I-CORDS, TWISTED CORDS, AND FRINGE

I-cords are formed with special 3-pronged gadgets, or simply by knitting a few stitches in the round with two double-pointed needles as follows:

Cast 3 sts onto one double-pointed needle. *Slide the sts to the opposite end of the needle and now hold the needle with sts in your left hand, with right side of work facing you. Draw the working yarn to the right behind the cast-on sts, and using the second needle, knit the 3 sts again. Repeat from * until the I-cord is the desired length, and as you work, be sure to draw the working yarn somewhat tightly across the back of the stitches so that an evenly rounded cord is formed.

Twisted cord is formed by cutting the number of suggested lengths of yarn indicated in the pattern and tying one end of the lengths together to a doorknob. Twist the other end

of the strands tightly, and when the twist feels sufficient fold the cord in half, letting it twist onto itself. Knot each end of cord to fasten, and trim ends.

Fringe is made by using the number and length of strands specified in the project. Holding the strands together evenly, fold them in half to make a loop. Insert a crochet hook into the garment where you plan to apply the fringe, and catch all the strands in the center. Draw the loop end through (photo 18), making it large enough so you can pull the ends of the yarn through the loop (photo 19). Pull down on the ends so the loops tighten snugly around the stitch.

Draw the loop through making it large enough for catching all the strands.

Pull down on the ends so the loops tighten snugly around the stitch.

CROCHET TRIM WITH BEADS

For attaching beads, use a very fine crochet hook, such as a size #11 steel crochet hook, for adding seed beads. Insert the crochet hook directly into the bead; it should be able to pass through easily. Then insert the crochet hook into the next stitch that is to be crocheted, and catch the working yarn. Draw the working yarn through the stitch and bead, forming a loop. Finish the crochet stitch as you normally would by placing the loop with the attached bead onto the larger crochet hook from the project (2.75mm/C crochet hook, in Sweetheart Cardigan, for instance).

DECORATIVE DUPLICATE CROCHET STITCH

The Soiree Skirt, pictured on page 110 utilizes a decorative duplicate crochet stitch.

Using a crochet hook and working yarn held behind work, carefully insert crochet hook from the right side of work into bottom hem and draw through a loop. On the right side, start to create a chain by inserting hook into knitted stitch in the first row and drawing through another loop, and in one continuous motion, drawing the new loop through the previous loop on the hook (one loop now remains on hook). Repeat the process by inserting the hook into the next stitch directly above to draw up the new loop. A visible raised chain will appear that is attached to the knitted garment.

PROVISIONAL CAST ON

This cast on is used in the Soho Overskirt on page 38 and the sleeves of Gwenivere's Choice Tunic on page 64.

Using crochet hook and scrap yarn in a contrasting color, chain enough stitches for the pattern, and then an additional 5 or so.

On one side the stitches form Vs (photo 20) while on the other side of the chain the stitches form the purl bumps (photo 21). Insert the knitting needle into the second purl

Crochet a chain with scrap yarn.

Turn chain over to identify purl bumps.

Insert the needle into each purl bump drawing up a loop through each purl bump.

bump next to the one forming the loop on hook (photo 22). Work chain, drawing up a loop in each following purl bump to pick up enough stitches to accommodate the number of stitches required by the pattern.

Now attach yarn and start to knit following the instructions for the project.

KNITTED CAST ON

This method allows you to add new stitches to existing stitches on the left-hand needle. If you do not already have any stitches on your needles, cast on 1 stitch by making a slip knot, or any way you wish, and hold the needle with the stitch in the left hand. Continue process as follows:

Insert the right-hand needle into the first stitch on the left-hand needle, as if to knit it. Knit the stitch, but do not drop the stitch from the left needle. Place the newly knitted stitch back on the left-hand needle (photo 23). Continue adding new stitches in this manner, until you have added as many stitches as the pattern calls for.

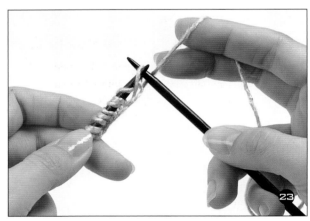

Knitted cast on to add new stitches to the needle.

Three-needle bind-off to attach two knitted pieces.

THREE-NEEDLE BIND-OFF

Three-needle bind-off is used to join two pieces together while binding off. This eliminates the need to sew seams. With wrong sides of the knitted fabric facing outward, hold two needles together. With a third needle, knit two stitches together, working one stitch from the front needle and one stitch from the back needle. ★Knit next two stitches together as before, taking one stitch from the front and one from the back. Pass the previous stitch worked over the latest stitch worked to bind off. Repeat from ★ until all stitches have been bound off.

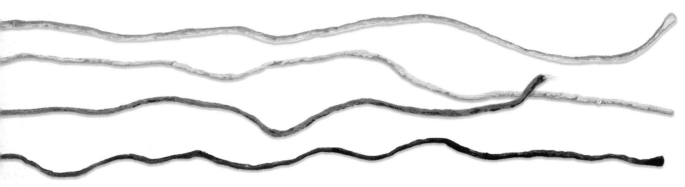

LACE-UP CLOSURE

This is used for Gwenivere's Choice Tunic shown on page 64 and the Faux Crochet Cropped Bolero on page 48. The garment is threaded like a shoelace along the front edge as follows:

Using a length of specified yarn, insert each end through top of piece from the right side, one through right front top edge, and one through left front top edge. Pull ends out so that they are equal in length. Cross the 2 ends in an X, then thread them through from the wrong side to the right side. Cross the 2 ends in an X again, then thread them through from the right side to the wrong side. Repeat this sequence until you are at the bottom edge. Tie remaining ends in a bow tie. Wear the garment by slipping it on over the head.

FINISHING

TIPS ON ASSEMBLING GARMENTS

Block all pieces before sewing them together. When working with soft and stretchy knitted garments, use the finest yarn used in the project to seam the pieces so it does not show. Make sure to sew side seams of garments before inserting sleeves.

CARE OF LUXURY FIBERS

It is best to hand-wash these garments carefully with a very mild soap specifically meant for fine washables. Do not wring them, but after soaking in a cool, mild soap bath and rinsing, roll them in a towel to absorb the excessive moisture, and carefully lay them on a flat surface to dry completely without being moved.

To block these yarns, use a hand steamer. If you do use an iron, make sure to place a protective cloth, such as a dish towel, between the hot iron and the knitted fabric.

Cast On—When no special cast on is specified in this book, a long tail cast on is assumed. Make a slip knot in your working yarn, leaving sufficient yarn for the number of cast on stitches specified by the pattern and work your way back toward the end as you form the stitches—the extra tail used in this method is the "long tail."

Cast Off—(also referred to as Bind Off). Bind off by knitting a stitch, then knitting the next stitch and passing the first knitted stitch over the second knitted stitch (a decrease of 1 stitch).

Double Long St—Knit stitch wrapping yarn three times around needle to form 3 loops. On following row, knit into first loop of triple wrap and drop second and third loops to form double elongated stitch.

Garter stitch—knit every row

inc—increase

Inc 1—Knit into front loop, then into back loop of same stitch (1 st increased)

K1tbl— Knit 1 stitch through back loop of stitch

K1tfl—Knit 1 stitch through front loop of stitch

K2tog—Knit two stitches together as if they were one (1 st decreased)

K3tog—Knit 3 stitches together as one (2 sts decreased)

LP—lace panel. Yo, sl 1, k2tog, psso, yo (3 sts worked over 3 sts)

Long st—Knit a stitch by wrapping yarn around needle twice (instead of once). On following row, knit just the first of the two wraps, letting the second one drop from needle to create a stitch twice as long as a regular stitch.

M1—Make one. With left needle tip, lift, connecting strand between last knit stitch on right needle and next stitch on left needle to form loop on left needle. Knit into back of this loop (1 st increased).

P2sso—Pass the 2 slipped stitches over the knitted stitch (2 sts decreased).

P2tog—Purl 2 stitches together as one (1 st decreased)

P3tog—Purl 3 stitches together as 1 (decrease of 2 sts)

PM—Place marker on needle

Psso—Pass slipped stitch over last worked stitch (decrease of 1 st)

Repeat from *—Repeat instructions following asterisk as many times as indicated, in addition to the first time.

RM—Remove marker

Round—Continuous row worked around on circular or double-pointed needles

RS—Right side of work

Short rows—Partial row is worked, then piece is turned and worked back to original edge; used for adding fullness to one section of piece.

SKP—Slip, knit, pass—Slip 1 stitch knitwise, knit next stitch, pass slipped stitch over knitted stitch (1 st decreased).

Sl 1—Slip 1 stitch knitwise (as though to knit)

Sl 1 wyib—Slip 1 stitch with yarn in back of work (on right-side rows)

Sl 1 wyif—Slip 1 stitch with yarn in front of work (on wrong-side rows)

Sl 2tog—Slip 2 stitches together with yarn in back as though to knit

SSK—Slip, slip, knit (decrease of 1 st)—Slip each of next 2 stitches knitwise to right needle, insert left needle into fronts of these stitches from left to right. Knit them together (1 st decreased).

SSP—Slip, slip, pass (decrease of 1 st). Slip first stitch knitwise, slip second stitch knitwise, pass first slipped stitch over second slipped stitch without knitting either stitch.

Stockinette st—Knit on right side rows, purl on wrong side rows.

st, sts—Stitch(es)

tbl—Through back loop

tfl—Through front loop

tog—Together

Turn—Transfer the left needle to the right hand and the right needle to the left hand, bringing the yarn up and over to the back between the tops of the two needles.

WS—Wrong side of work

wyib—With yarn in back of work

wyif—With yarn in front of work

yo—Yarn over. Bring yarn forward under right needle tip and wrap it front to back over needle to form loop over needle, adding 1 stitch. On following row, work this added loop as a stitch.

yo twice—Yarn over twice (2 wraps). On following row, knit into front loop, then into back loop of double wrap (2 sts increased).

CHAPTER 1

The projects in this chapter are perfect for those starting out with lace. You'll learn to easily create faux lace with finer yarn and long stitches, be introduced to a pretty 6-stitch lace pattern, and learn how an airy, openwork stitch pattern is accomplished through a simple 2-stitch repeat.

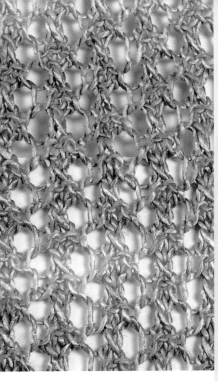

After Five Lace Shrug

EXPERIENCE LEVEL

Easy

SIZES

Small/medium, (large/extra large)

T HIS LIGHTWEIGHT SHORT OR LONG-SLEEVED SHRUG WILL ADD ELEGANCE AND ROMANCE TO ANY OUTFIT. WEAR IT OVER ANY SLEEVELESS GARMENT AND FEEL BATHED IN THE SOFT SILKINESS OF THE KNITTED FABRIC.

FINISHED MEASUREMENTS

About 43"/109cm (50"/127cm) long (sleeve edge to sleeve edge) and 16"/40.5cm (20½"/52cm) wide (from top edge to lower edge at center back), lying flat and unstretched. Because of lace pattern, piece can be stretched in length or in width.

MATERIALS

Approx total: 489yd/447m (652yd/596m) silk lightweight yarn

Knitting needles: 5mm (size 8 U.S.)
or size to obtain gauge

Tapestry needle for finishing

GAUGE

16 sts and 22 rows = 4"/10cm in Trellis Lace pattern
Always take time to check your gauge.

PATTERN STITCH

Trellis Lace

(pattern from *The Harmony Guides, 450 Knitting Stitches,* Volume 2, page 51)

(Multiple of 6 sts, plus 5)

Row 1 (RS): K4, ★yo, sl 1, k2tog, psso, yo, k3; repeat from ★ across to last st, k1.

Row 2: K1, p to last st, k1.

Row 3: K1, ★yo, sl 1, k2tog, psso, yo, k3: repeat from ★ across to last 4 sts, yo, sl 1, k2tog, psso, yo, k1.

Row 4: K1, p to last st, k1.

Repeat these 4 rows for lace pattern.

INSTRUCTIONS

SHRUG

Starting at one sleeve edge, cast on 65 (83) sts. Work in Trellis Lace pattern, working 10 (13) pattern repeats across, until piece measures 43"/109cm (50"/127cm) from beginning.

Bind off all sts. Cut yarn. Weave in ends.

FINISHING

At each end of piece, fold side edges in to meet at center to form sleeve. With right sides together, seam these edges together, starting at sleeve edge, for about 9½"/24cm adjusting length of seam as needed to accommodate various sizes.

This project was knit with 3 (4) skeins of Artyarns Regal Silk, 100% silk lightweight yarn, 1.8oz/50g = 163yd/149m per skein, color #137, variegated beige.

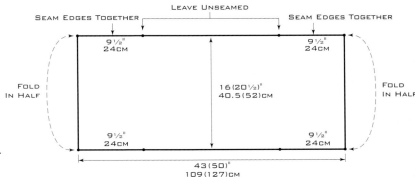

Tulle-Trimmed Top

■

EXPERIENCE LEVEL

Easy

SIZES

X-Small (Small, Medium, Large)

LOOKING FOR A SHOW-STOPPING, ULTRA-FEMININE TOP? TAKE A SCRAP OF DRESSY FABRIC, SUCH AS TULLE, AND KNIT RIGHT ONTO IT TO MAKE A FLUID, OFF-THE-SHOULDER NECKLINE. EASY TO KNIT, THIS PIECE USES FINER YARN FOR WAIST SHAPING. NO SEAMING IS REQUIRED.

FINISHED MEASUREMENTS

Note: Measurements given below are for when this form-fitting garment is actually worn, and include about 10" inches of stretching. The garment, lying flat and unstretched, will measure only about 22 (24, 26, 28)"/56 (61, 66, 71)cm at bust.

Bust: 32 (34, 36, 38)"/81 (86, 91, 96.5)cm

Total length: About 15 (15½, 16, 16½)"/38 (39.5, 40.5, 42)cm

Snug fit

MATERIALS

Approx total: 326 (489, 489, 652)yd/298 (447, 447, 596)m silk lightweight yarn (yarn A) and

230yd/210m mohair/silk blend superfine yarn (yarn B)

About 1½ yd/1.4m long strip of 9"/23cm wide tulle mesh

Circular needle: 4mm (size 6 U.S.)
or size to obtain gauge, 24"/61cm long

Crochet hook: 2.25mm (size B/1 U.S.)

Stitch markers

Stitch holders

GAUGE

20 sts and 28 rows = 4"/10cm in Stockinette Stitch

Always take time to check your gauge.

PATTERN STITCH

Stockinette Stitch in rounds

Knit every round.

Stockinette Stitch in rows

Row 1 (RS): Knit.

Row 2: Purl.

Repeat these 2 rows.

INSTRUCTIONS

TOP

Note: This top is knitted from the top down.

Holding edge of tulle strip and starting along one long edge about 8"/20cm from end, work as follows:

With yarn B held behind tulle strip, gently insert crochet hook through strip to pull through a yarn loop, working about ¼"/7.75mm in from edge of tulle; place loop on circular needle. Repeat along tulle strip edge, pulling through a total of 156 (170, 186, 202) stitches evenly spaced across (see note below) and leaving 8"/20cm free at opposite end of strip.

Note: To make it easier to space the sts evenly, leave 8"/20cm free at each end and fold remainder of tulle strip in half, then in half again and mark each fold with a pin; work a quarter of the stitches in each quarter section of strip.

Join stitches on needle, being carefully not to twist sts around needle. Mark beginning of rounds. Working in Stockinette Stitch in rounds on circular needle, knit 5 rounds. Cut B and attach A.

With A, knit 9 rounds.

Divide work for armhole shaping

Next round: Continuing with A, k 44 (48, 53, 57) sts for front, bind off next 34 (37, 40, 44) sts for top section of armhole, k until there are 44 (48, 53, 57) sts on needle for back, bind off remaining 34 (37, 40, 44) sts for top of other armhole. Now work back and forth in rows on circular needle, working on front sts only.

FRONT

Row 1 (RS): With A, k44 (48, 53, 57) sts of front.

Row 2: With A, p44 (48, 53, 57).

Repeat these last 2 rows 4 times more.

Place these 44 (48, 53, 57) front sts on a stitch holder. Cut yarn.

BACK

With right side of work facing you, attach yarn to back stitches remaining on needle and work rows same as for the front sts. Turn work.

Next row (RS): Using knitted cast-on method, cast on 12 (13, 14, 15) sts for underarm, knit across these cast-on sts and the back sts; turn work and cast on 12 (13, 14, 15) sts for second underarm, turn work back to RS, place front stitches from holder onto left needle tip with RS side facing you, knit across front sts - 112 (122, 134, 144) sts.

Join first and last stitches and work in Stockinette Stitch in rounds until piece measures 3 (3½, 4, 4½)"/7.5 (9, 10, 11.5)cm from armhole cast-on edge.

Attach yarn B and alternately knit 2 rows with B and rows with A until fifth B stripe is completed. Cut B. Continue knitting with A only, until piece measures 15 (15½, 16, 16½)"/38 (39.5, 40.5, 42) from top knitted row to bottom, measuring at center front.

FINISHING

Bind off with crochet hook as follows:

Cut A and attach B. With B work ★single crochet (sc) into each of 2 sts, work 3 sc in next st; repeat from ★ around entire edge. Cut B and fasten off. Weave in yarn ends.

With B, crochet a row of sc around each armhole, spacing sts to keep edge smooth and flat.

This project was knit with 2 (3, 3, 4) skeins of Artyarns Regal Silk, 100% silk lightweight yarn, 1.8oz/50g = 163yd/149m per skein, color #252, navy (yarn A) and 1 skein of Artyarns Silk Mohair, 70% mohair/30% silk blend superfine yarn, .9oz/25g = 230yd/210m per skein, color #123, variegated sea greens (yarn B).

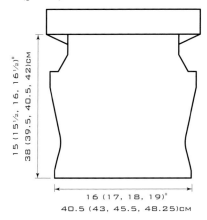

15 (15½, 16, 16½)"
38 (39.5, 40.5, 42)CM

16 (17, 18, 19)"
40.5 (43, 45.5, 48.25)CM

Gatsby Trellis Hat

![swatch]

EXPERIENCE LEVEL
Easy

SIZES
One size fits most.

Gatsby Trellis Hat

DON THIS SLEEK TOPPER AND ADD INSTANT DRAMA TO ANY HAIRSTYLE. FASHIONING IT OUT OF INCREDIBLY SOFT MERINO ENSURES LIGHTWEIGHT COMFORT IN ANY SEASON.

FINISHED MEASUREMENTS

About 19"/48cm in circumference, unstretched, and 6"/15cm from center top to outer edge.

MATERIALS

Approx total: 188yd/172m wool medium-weight yarn (yarn A,) and

191yd/175m wool superfine (fingering) weight yarn (yarn B)

Circular needles: 5mm (size 8 U.S.) or size to obtain gauge, 16"/40.5cm long

Set (4) double-pointed needles: 5mm (size 8 U.S.) *or size to obtain gauge*

Crochet hook: 2.25mm (size B/1 U.S.)

Stitch marker

Tapestry needle

GAUGE

14 sts and 24 rows = 4"/10cm in Garter Stitch with yarn A

Always take time to check your gauge.

PATTERN STITCH

Garter Stitch in rounds

Round 1: Knit around.

Round 2: Purl around.

Repeat these 2 rounds.

Long Stitch

Knit each stitch wrapping yarn two times around needle to form 2 loops. On following row knit into first loop and drop second loop to form elongated stitch.

INSTRUCTIONS

CAP

Starting at outer edge of cap, using circular needle and with 1 strand each of yarns A and B held together, cast on 64 sts. Join to work in rounds, being careful not to twist sts around needle. Place a marker on needle to mark beginning of rounds; slip marker on each round.

Round 1: With A and B, p64. Drop A.

Round 2: With B only, work Long sts (page 8) to marker. Drop B and pick up A. Throughout, carry strand of unused yarn loosely on wrong side of work up to next round where it is needed.

Round 3: With A only, p to marker, dropping second wrap of each st to form long sts.

Round 4: With A, k to marker.

Round 5: With A, p to marker.

Rounds 6 through 17: Repeat Rounds 2 through 5 for 3 times more.

TOP SHAPING

Change to double-pointed needles and continue to slip marker at end of rounds.

Round 18: With A and B, *k2tog, k6; repeat from * 7 times more—56 sts. Work with A and B held together for remainder of top.

Round 19 and all following odd-numbered rounds: P to marker.

Round 20: *K2tog, k5; repeat from * 7 times more—48 sts.

Round 22: *K2tog, k4; repeat from * 7 times more—40 sts.

Round 24: *K2tog, k3; repeat from * 7 times more—32 sts.

Round 26: *K2tog, k2; repeat from * 7 times more—24 sts.

Round 28: *K2tog, k1; repeat from * 7 times more—16 sts.

Round 30: *K2tog; repeat from * 7 times more—8 sts.

Round 31: Repeat Round 19.

Cut yarns, leaving an end (of A and B each) for finishing. Thread ends into tapestry needle and draw through remaining 8 sts. Draw sts tightly together and fasten off securely. Weave in ends.

FINISHING

With crochet hook and yarn B, crochet a round of single crochet (sc) around outer edge of cap, working a stitch in each cast-on st and being careful to work just loosely enough to maintain an edge that will fit around head.

Next round: Work *sc in each of next 2 sc of previous round, then work (sc, chain 3, sc) all in next sc; repeat from * around. Join to first sc with a crocheted slip stitch. Fasten off and weave in ends.

This project was knit with 1 skein of Artyarns Ultramerino 8, 100% Merino wool medium-weight yarn, 3.5oz/100g = 188yd/172m per skein, color #250, cream (yarn A), and

1 skein of Artyarns Ultramerino 4, 100% Merino wool superfine (fingering) weight yarn, 1.8oz/50g = 191yd/175m per skein, color #250, cream (yarn B).

Four Rectangle Sweater

EXPERIENCE LEVEL
Easy

SIZES
X-Small (Small, Medium, Large)

It's hard to believe that this form-fitting sweater is made with just four simple rectangles. The vertical panels running down each side are not only attractive design elements, but serve to make the top visually slimming.

FINISHED GARMENT MEASUREMENTS

Bust: 31 (35, 39, 43)"/ 79 (89, 99, 109)cm

Standard Fit

MATERIALS

Approx total: 624 (728, 832, 938)yd/571 (666, 761, 858)m Merino wool medium-weight yarn (yarn A), and

Approx total: 414 (552, 690, 690)yd/379 (505, 631, 631)m ⅛"/3mm-wide silk ribbon (yarn B)

Knitting needles: 4.5mm (size 7 U.S.)
or size to obtain gauge

Extra needle, same size, for 3-needle bind off

Tapestry needle for finishing

GAUGE

18½ sts and 29 rows = 4"/10cm in Daisy Pattern Stitch

Always take time to check your gauge.

PATTERN STITCH

Daisy Pattern

Rows 1 and 2: With A, k across over both rows. Drop A; attach B. Carry yarn not in use loosely along side edge of work as you proceed.

Row 3 (RS): With B, ★k1, k3tog through front loops and leave the original 3 sts on the left needle, then working on these same 3 sts, k3tog through the back loops, then k3tog through the front loops again (k3tog worked 3 times over the same 3 stitches) and then remove the original 3 sts from the left needle; rep from ★ across, ending k1.

Row 4: With B, k1, p to last st, k1. Drop B; pick up A.

Rows 5 and 6: With A, k across over both rows. Drop A; pick up B.

Repeat Rows 3 through 6 to continue in pattern.

Four Rectangle Sweater

INSTRUCTIONS

BACK

With yarn A, cast on 69 (81, 89, 97) sts.

Work in Daisy Pattern until piece measures 18 (19½, 21, 22½)"/45.5 (49.5, 53.5, 57)cm. Bind off all sts with A, using Loose Cast-off Method in Basics Section, page 15.

FRONT

Work same as for back.

SLEEVES

Make 2.

With A, cast on 45 (57, 65, 73) sts.

Work in Daisy Pattern until sleeve measures 19½ (20, 20½, 21)"/49.5 (51, 52, 53.5)cm

Bind off all sts with A.

FINISHING

Mark the bound-off edges of the front and back 22 (26, 28, 30) sts in from each arm edge for shoulders, leaving 25 (29, 33, 37) center sts for neck opening. With right sides of front and back together, seam each shoulder from arm edge to marker. Turn right side out.

Underarm gusset

Leaving top 5 (6, 7, 8)"/12.5 (15, 17.5, 20)cm unworked for armhole opening and using yarn B, pick up and k 61 (65, 69, 73) sts evenly spaced along one underarm edge (working about 2 sts in every A ridge and 1 st in every B ridge). K 12 (14, 16, 18) rows. Cut yarn, leaving sts on needle.

At the same underarm, with B and right side of work facing you, using extra needle, start at lower edge to pick up and k 61 (65, 69, 73) sts along matching edge. Then with wrong sides facing you, using 3-needle bind-off, bind off the newly picked up sts and the previously worked gusset sts together for underarm seam.

Repeat underarm gusset on other side of garment.

Sleeve gusset

With right side facing you, using A, pick up and k 76 (78, 80, 82) sts along one long sleeve edge (working about 1 st each ridge). Attach B and k 2 rows. Alternating A and B, k 2 rows once more. Cut A, leaving sts on needle. On opposite side of sleeve, with right side of work facing you and using A, pick up and k 76 (78, 80, 82) sts. With wrong sides facing you, using 3-needle bind-off, bind off all sts to seam sleeve.

Repeat on other sleeve.

With right sides together, sew a sleeve to each armhole opening.

Weave in yarn ends.

This project was knit with 6 (7, 8, 9) skeins of Artyarns Supermerino, 100% Merino Wool medium-weight yarn, 1.8oz/50g = 104yd/95m per skein, color #229 blue (yarn A,) and 3 (4, 5, 5) skeins Artyarns Silk Ribbon, ⅛"/3mm-wide 100% silk ribbon, .9oz/25g = 138yd/126m per skein, color #229 blue.

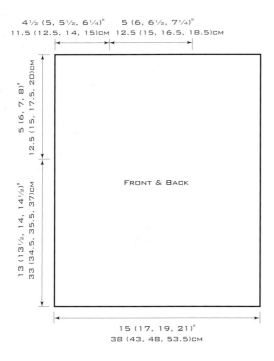

4½ (5, 5½, 6¼)"
11.5 (12.5, 14, 15)cm

5 (6, 6½, 7¼)"
12.5 (15, 16.5, 18.5)cm

5 (6, 7, 8)"
12.5 (15, 17.5, 20)cm

13 (13½, 14, 14½)"
33 (34.5, 35.5, 37)cm

FRONT & BACK

15 (17, 19, 21)"
38 (43, 48, 53.5)cm

19½ (20, 20½, 21)"
49.5 (51, 52, 53.5)cm

SLEEVE

9½ (11½, 13½, 15)"
24 (29, 34, 38)cm

Soho Overskirt

EXPERIENCE LEVEL

Intermediate

SIZE

Small (Medium, Large, X-Large)

GO A LITTLE BOHEMIAN AND SLIP THIS SAUCY OVERSKIRT OVER A SATIN SHIFT OF ANY COLOR FOR A KICKY, LAYERED LOOK. USE SINGLE AND DOUBLE ELONGATED STITCHES TO CREATE A SLIGHT FLARE AT THE HEM IN THIS SIDE-TO-SIDE KNIT.

FINISHED MEASUREMENTS

Note: Measurements given below are for when this form-fitting garment is actually worn, and include up to 12" of stretching. The garment, lying flat and unstretched, will measure only about 28 (30, 32, 34)"/71 (76, 81.5, 86.5)cm at hips. Length of skirt will shorten slightly as skirt is stretched sideways.

Waist: 32 (34, 36, 38)"/ 81 (86, 91.5, 96.5)cm without drawstring

Hips: 35 (37, 41, 45)"/89 (94, 104, 114)cm

Bottom edge: 42 (44, 47, 52)"/106.5 (111.5, 119.5, 132)cm

Length (unstretched): 19 (22, 24, 26)"/ 48 (56, 61, 66)cm

Snug fit

MATERIALS

Approx total: 188 (376, 376, 564)yd/172 (344, 344, 516)m Merino wool medium-weight yarn (yarn A), and 255 (255, 510, 510)yd/233 (233, 467, 467)m cashmere 2-ply superfine (fingering) yarn (yarn B)

Knitting needles: 4.5mm (size 7 U.S.)
or size to obtain gauge

Extra needle (same size as above) for binding off

Scrap yarn for provisional cast-on

Crochet hook: 2.75mm (size C/2 U.S.)

Stitch marker

Stitch holder

Tapestry needle for finishing

4 small round beads, about ¼"/6mm in diameter

GAUGE

14 sts and 24 rows = 4"/10cm in Garter Stitch
Always take time to check your gauge.

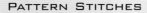
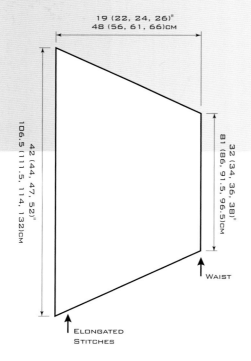

PATTERN STITCHES

Garter Stitch

Knit every row.

Long Stitch

Knit each stitch wrapping yarn two times around needle to form 2 loops. On following row knit into first loop and drop second loop to form elongated stitch.

Double Long Stitch

Knit each stitch wrapping yarn three times around needle to form 3 loops. On following row knit into first loop and drop second loop to form double-elongated stitch.

Openwork Stitch

(Even number of sts)

Row 1: K1, *yo, SKP; repeat from * to last st, k1.

Elongated Panel

Rows 1 and 2: Starting at bottom edge, with A, work Openwork St Pattern.

Rows 3 and 4: With B, knit across.

Row 5: With B, knit Long St on 50 sts, k to end.

Row 6: With B, k to end, knitting into only the first wrap of each long stitch and dropping remaining wrap.

Rows 7 and 8: With A, work Openwork St Pattern to end.

Rows 9 and 10: With B, knit across.

Rows 11 and 12: With A, work Openwork St Pattern.

Rows 13 and 14: With B, knit across.

Rows 15 and 16: Repeat Rows 5 and 6.

Rows 17 and 18: With A, work Openwork St Pattern.

Rows 19 and 20: With B, knit across.

These 20 rows form Long St Panel.

Double Elongated Panel

Row 1: Starting at bottom edge with yarn B, knit Double Long St on 29 sts, knit Long St on 22 sts, k to end (waist edge). (See Basics page 8.)

Row 2: With B, k to end, knitting into only the first wrap of each elongated stitch and dropping remaining wrap(s).

Rows 3 and 4: With A, work Openwork St Pattern to end.

Rows 5 and 6: With B, knit across.

Rows 7 and 8: Repeat Rows 1 and 2.

These 8 rows form Double Elongated Panel.

INSTRUCTIONS

Note: This skirt is knitted from side to side, with rows worked back and forth between waist and bottom edge. Be sure to carry the yarn not in use carefully along edge of work, leaving it just loose enough not to draw up edge, but not so loose as to cause a loopy hem edge. When carrying a yarn more than 2 rows at a time, twist yarns at end of row to catch carried yarn in place. When changing colors, bring carried yarn up from underneath worked yarn to begin new yarn. (See

Diagram labels:
19 (22, 24, 26)"
48 (56, 61, 66)CM

42 (44, 47, 52)"
106.5 (111.5, 114, 132)CM

32 (34, 36, 38)"
81 (86, 91.5, 96.5)CM

WAIST

ELONGATED STITCHES

page 18, "Carrying two yarns up along side of work.")

With A, using provisional cast-on method (see page 19), cast on 66 (78, 84, 90) sts. Work as follows:

With B, knit 2 rows.

Then work 20 rows of Elongated Panel, followed by 8 rows of Double Elongated Panel. Continue to work, alternating the two panels, until piece measures about 32 (34, 36, 38)"/ 81 (86, 91.5, 96.5)cm at waist edge (narrow edge), when slightly stretched.

FINISHING

Bind off as follows:

Remove scrap yarn from provisional cast-on and place sts on needle. Fold skirt in half with right sides together, and wrong side facing, and needles with sts of cast-on row and last row held together. Using extra needle, work 3-needle bind-off (see page 20) to attach these 2 rows of sts together, joining side edges of skirt.

DRAWSTRING

Cut a 4yd/3.5m length of yarn A. Make a twisted cord (see page 18) about 46 to 50"/117 to 127cm long. Knot each end. Weave cord in and out of top row of eyelets at waist for drawstring. Thread a strand of B yarn in tapestry needle and knot one end. Thread a bead onto thread and push it down to the knot. Draw needle with thread through one end of drawstring, letting bead dangle 2"/5cm, knot thread at drawstring, then draw thread through another bead pushing it up to 2"/5cm from drawstring, and knot bead securely in place. Trim off excess thread. Repeat on other end of drawstring with remaining 2 beads.

This project was knit with 1 (2, 2, 3) skeins of Artyarns Ultramerino 8, 100% Merino wool medium-weight yarn, 3½ oz/100g = 188yd/172m per skein, color #253, pale pink (yarn A), and

1 (1, 2, 2) skeins Artyarns Cashmere 2, 100% cashmere 2-ply superfine (fingering) yarn, 1.8 oz/50g = 255yd/233m per skein, color #253, pale pink (yarn B).

BONUS PROJECT

WANT MORE USING THIS TECHNIQUE?
VISIT WWW.ARTYARNS.COM

Sweetheart Cardigan

EXPERIENCE LEVEL

Intermediate

SIZE

Small (Medium, Large, X-Large)

There's no denying that this cardi with its ruffles, gauzy knitted fabric, and beaded trim is the epitome of femininity. To narrow any waistline, this light-as-mist piece is belted with a silken I-cord tie.

FINISHED GARMENT MEASUREMENTS

Bust: About 37 (39, 41, 43)"/94 (99, 104, 109)cm

Total length: 23 (23¾, 24½, 25¼)"/58.5 (60, 62, 64)cm

Standard Fit

MATERIALS

Approx total: 460 (460, 690, 690)yd/421 (421, 631, 631)m mohair and silk blend superfine weight yarn, for each of 2 different, but closely related, colors (color A and color B), and

Approx total: 138yd/126m of ⅛"/3mm-wide silk ribbon for I-cord belt.

Knitting needles: 4.5mm (size 7 U.S.) *or size to obtain gauge*

Crochet hook: 2.75mm (size C/2 U.S.)

Stitch marker

Stitch holder

3 buttons, about ½"/1.3mm in diameter

For beading trim (optional): Approx 100 seed beads, and steel crochet hook: Size 11 (1.1mm), or fine enough to fit through beads

GAUGE

17 sts and 26 rows = 4"/10cm in Knit and Purl Panel

Always take time to check your gauge.

PATTERN STITCHES

Knit and Purl Panel

Note: Drop color not in use until needed again. Always carry color not in use loosely up side of work to where it is needed again.

Row 1 (RS): With color A, k across.

Row 2: With A, k1, purl to last st, k1,

Row 3: With color B, k1, purl to last st, k1.

Row 4: With B, k across.

Repeat these 4 rows for pattern.

Work 12 rows (3 pattern repeats) to form a panel.

Openwork Panel

(Even number of sts)

Row 1: With a strand each of colors A and B held together, k1, *yo, SKP; repeat from * to last st, k1.

Repeat Row 1 for pattern.

Work 8 rows to form a panel.

Sweetheart Cardigan

INSTRUCTIONS

BACK

With 1 strand each of colors A and B held together, cast on 154 (162, 170, 182) sts for bottom edge. Work 12 rows for Knit and Purl Panel.

Next row: With A and B held together, k1, *k2tog; repeat from * to last st, k1—78 (82, 86, 92) sts.

Continue to work as follows: Work 8 rows of Openwork Panel, with A and B held together, then 12 rows of Knit and Purl Panel, alternating colors.

Work even until piece measures 14½ (15, 15½, 16)"/37 (38, 39, 40.5)cm.

Armhole shaping

Continuing to alternate panel patterns as before, bind off 4 sts at beginning of next 2 rows, then bind off 3 sts at beginning of next 2 rows. Decrease 1 st at beginning and end of every other row 3 (3, 4, 4) times—58 (62, 64, 70) sts.

Work even until armholes measure 8½ (8¾, 9, 9¼)"/21.5 (22, 23, 23.5)cm.

Bind off all sts for shoulders and neck.

LEFT FRONT

With 1 strand each of colors A and B held together, cast on 78 (82, 86, 90) sts. Work 12 rows for Knit and Purl Panel.

Next row: With A and B held together, k1, *k2tog; repeat from * to last st, k1—40 (42, 44, 46) sts.

Work in alternating panel patterns as for back until front measures same length (and same pattern row) as back to armhole.

Armhole and neck shaping

At armhole edge, bind off 4 sts once, then 3 sts every other row once. At same edge, decrease 1 st every other row 3 (3, 4, 4) times, and at the same time, on the 6th row of armhole shaping, at neck edge bind off 14 (14, 15, 15) sts once—16 (18, 18, 20) sts remain when armhole shaping is completed.

Work even until piece measures same as back to shoulder. Bind off all sts.

RIGHT FRONT

Work to correspond to left front, reversing all shaping.

SLEEVES

Make 2.

With 1 strand each of colors A and B held together, cast on 50 (54, 58, 62) sts. Work 12 rows of Knit and Purl Panel.

Next row: With A and B held together, k1, *k2tog; repeat from * to last st, k1—26 (28, 30, 32) sts.

Work in alternating panel patterns as for back and, at the same time, increase 1 st at the beginning and end of every 4th row 9 (10, 12, 13) times, then every 6th row 9 (9, 8, 8) times—62 (66, 70, 74) sts.

Continuing patterns, work even until sleeve measures 16 (16½, 17, 17½)"/40.5 (42, 43, 44.5)cm from beginning.

Sleeve cap shaping

Bind off 4 sts at beginning of next 2 rows, then bind off 3 sts at beginning of next 2 rows. Decrease 1 st at beginning and end of every other row 3 (4, 4, 5) times—42 (44, 48, 50) sts. Then decrease 1 st at beginning and end of every 3rd row 10 (11, 11, 12) times. Bind off 4 (4, 5, 5) sts at beginning of next 2 rows. Bind off remaining 14 (14, 16, 16) sts.

FINISHING

With right sides of back and each front together, sew shoulder and side seams, aligning panel patterns at side edges. Sew underarm seams of sleeves; turn sleeves right side out. With right sides together, pin a sleeve to each armhole, matching sleeve seam to side seams and center top of sleeve cap to shoulder seams. Sew sleeves in place.

Note: See Crochet Trim with Beads on page 19.

With size 11 crochet hook and color A yarn, crochet edging around bottom, neck, and sleeve edges as follows:

★Work single crochet (sc) in next 2 sts, sc with bead, sc in next st; repeat from ★ along entire edge, spacing sts to keep edge smooth and flat.

I-cord belt

Note: See I-cord on page 18.

With silk ribbon, make an I-cord 70"/178cm long, allowing 6"/15cm of unworked ribbon to hang free at each end of cord.

Weave the cord in and out of the Openwork Panel at waist. Tie cord ends in a bow when cardigan is worn.

Buttons

Sew 3 buttons, evenly spaced along left front edge near center of top 3 Openwork panels.

The eyelets in the corresponding panels along the right front will serve as the buttonholes.

This project was worked with 2 (2, 3, 3) skeins of Artyarns Silk Mohair, 70% mohair/30% silk blend superfine yarn, .9oz/25g = 230yd/210m per skein, color #407, variegated pink (color A), and

2 (2, 3, 3) skeins of Artyarns Silk Mohair, 70% mohair/30% silk blend superfine yarn, .9oz/25g = 230yd/210m per skein, color #405, variegated peach (color B), and

1 skein Artyarns Silk Ribbon, ⅛"/3mm-wide 100% silk ribbon, .9oz/25g = 138yd/126m per skein, color #215, pink.

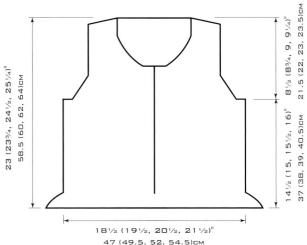

23 (23¾, 24¼, 25¼)"
58.5 (60, 62, 64)CM

8½ (8¾, 9, 9¼)"
21.5 (22, 23, 23.5)CM

14½ (15, 15½, 16)"
37 (38, 39, 40.5)CM

18½ (19½, 20½, 21½)"
47 (49.5, 52, 54.5)CM

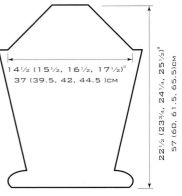

14½ (15½, 16½, 17½)"
37 (39.5, 42, 44.5)CM

22½ (23¾, 24¼, 25½)"
57 (60, 61.5, 65.5)CM

Simple Faux Lace and Lace All-Over Patterns

This chapter focuses on stitches whose looks defy that of conventional knitting. Learn how to knit unique lace that bears an uncanny resemblance to crochet, stitches that seemingly float in air, and lace of gossamer fineness and intricacy.

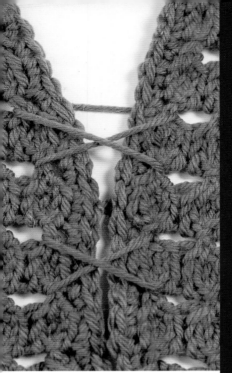

Faux Crochet Cropped Bolero

EXPERIENCE LEVEL

Intermediate

SIZES

Small/Medium (Large)

*D*ON'T KNOW HOW TO CROCHET? YOU DON'T HAVE TO. IT TAKES A KEEN EYE TO DISCERN THAT THIS CHIC LITTLE BOLERO IS ACTUALLY KNITTED. IT'S KNIT ALL IN ONE PIECE, STARTING AT THE BACK, WORKING OVER THE SHOULDERS, AND THEN ON DOWN THE FRONT PANELS.

FINISHED GARMENT MEASUREMENTS

Bust: About 32 (38)"/81 (96.5)cm at bust

Total length: 14½ (15¼)"/37 (38.5)cm

Snug fit

MATERIALS

Approx total: 312 (416)yd/285 (381)m Merino wool medium–weight yarn

Knitting needles: 4.5mm (size 7 U.S.)
or size to obtain gauge

Crochet hook: 2.75mm (size C/2 U.S.)

Tapestry needle for finishing

Stitch holder

GAUGE

18 sts and 24 rows = 4"/10cm in Pattern Stitch

Always take time to check your gauge.

PATTERN STITCHES

Triple St

(Worked over 3 sts)

SSP, transfer remaining stitch back to left needle; pass second stitch on left needle over the first, then work (k1tfl, k1tbl, k1tfl) all in the first stitch on left needle.

Triple Rib St

(Worked over 3 sts)

SSP, transfer remaining stitch back to left needle; pass second stitch on left needle over the first, then work (k1, p1, k1) all in the first st on left needle.

INSTRUCTIONS

BACK

Starting at lower edge of back, cast on 77 (89) sts.

Row 1 (RS): K2, *p1, k2; repeat from * across.

Row 2: K1, p1, k1, *p2, k1; repeat from * across to last 2 sts, p1, k1.

Rows 3 and 4: Repeat Rows 1 and 2.

Row 5: K1, *work Triple St over next 3 sts; repeat from * across to last st, k1.

Row 6: K1, p to last st, k1.

Row 7: K across.

Row 8: Repeat Row 6.

Repeat Rows 5 through 8 for 5 (6) times more, then repeat Rows 5 and 6 once more.

Armhole shaping

Row 1 (RS): Bind off 3 sts, k to end.

Row 2: Bind off 3 sts, p to end.

Row 3: Bind off 3 sts, work Triple St to last st, k1.

Row 4: Bind off 3 sts, p to end.

Row 5: K across.

Row 6: K1, p to last st, k1.

Rows 7 and 8: Repeat Rows 3 and 4—59 (71) sts remain.

Row 9: K across.

Row 10: K1, p to last st, k1.

Row 11: K1, work Triple St to last st, k1.

Row 12: Repeat row 10.

Repeat Rows 9 through 12 for 8 times more, then repeat Rows 9 and 10 once more.

Divide for neck opening and shoulders

Next row (RS): K1, work Triple St 5 (6) times, k1, place these 17 (20) sts on a stitch holder to be worked later for right front, then bind off center 25 (31) sts for back neck edge, k1, work Triple St 5 (6) times, k1—17 (20) sts remain for shoulder edge of left front.

LEFT FRONT

Row 1 (WS): K1, p to last st, k1.

Row 2: K across.

Row 3: K1, p to last st, k1.

Row 4: K1, work Triple St 5 (6) times, k1.

Neck shaping

Row 5: K1, p to end and using Knitted Cast-on (see page 20), cast on 3 sts (at neck edge).

Rows 6 and 7: Repeat Rows 2 and 3.

Row 8: K1, work Triple St 6 (7) times, k1.

Row 9: Repeat Row 1.

Rows 10 through 12: Repeat Rows 6 through 8.

Row 13: Repeat Row 5.

Rows 14 and 15: Repeat Rows 2 and 3.

Row 16: K1, work Triple St 7 (8) times, k1.

Row 17: Repeat Row 1.

Rows 18 through 20: Repeat Rows 14 through 16.

Row 21: Repeat Row 5.

Rows 22 through 23: Repeat Rows 2 and 3 once.

Row 24: K1, work Triple St 8 (9) times, k1.

Rows 25 through 27: Repeat Rows 1 through 3.

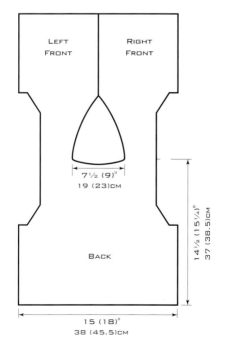

LEFT FRONT   RIGHT FRONT

7 ½ (9)"
19 (23)CM

14½ (15¼)"
37 (38.5)CM

BACK

15 (18)"
38 (45.5)CM

Row 28: Repeat Row 24.

Row 29: Repeat Row 5.

Rows 30 and 31: Repeat Rows 2 and 3.

Row 32: K1, work Triple St 9 (10) times, k1.

Rows 33 through 35: Repeat Rows 1 through 3.

Row 36: K1, work Triple St 9 (10) times, k1.

Row 37: Repeat Row 1.

Armhole shaping

Row 38: K across and using Knitted Cast-on, cast on 3 sts (arm edge).

Row 39: Repeat Row 1.

Row 40: K1, work Triple St 10 (11) times, k1.

Rows 41 through 43: Repeat Rows 37 through 39—35 (38) sts on Row 43.

Row 44: K1, work Triple St 11 (12) times, k1.

Rows 45 through 47: Repeat Rows 1 through 3.

Repeat Rows 44 through 47 for 7 (8) times more.

Ribbing

Row 1 (RS): K1, work Triple Rib St 11 (12) times, k1.

Row 2: P2, ★k1, p2; repeat from ★ across.

Row 3: K2, ★p1, k2; repeat from ★ across.

Repeat Rows 2 and 3 once more. Bind off all sts in ribbing pattern. Cut yarn.

RIGHT FRONT

Transfer right front stitches from holder back onto needle and attach yarn to neck edge of last row worked.

Row 1 (WS): K1, p to last st, k1.

Row 2: K across.

Row 3: K1, p to last st, k1.

Row 4: K1, work Triple St 5 (6) times, k1.

Row 5: K1, p to last st, k1.

Neck shaping

Row 6: K across and using Knitted Cast-on, cast on 3 sts (at neck edge).

Row 7: Repeat Row 3.

Row 8: K1, work Triple St 6 (7) times, k1.

Rows 9 through 11: Repeat Rows 1 through 3.

Row 12: Repeat Row 8.

Rows 13 through 15: Repeat Rows 5 through 7.

Row 16: K1, work Triple St 7 (8) times, k 1.

Rows 17 through 19: Repeat Rows 1 through 3.

Row 20: Repeat Row 16.

Rows 21 through 23: Repeat Rows 5 through 7.

Row 24: K1, work Triple St 8 (9) times, k 1.

Rows 25 through 27: Repeat Rows 1 through 3.

Row 28: Repeat Row 24.

Rows 29 and 30: Repeat rows 5 and 6.

Row 31: Repeat Row 3.

Row 32: K1, work Triple St 9 (10) times, k1.

Rows 33 through 34: Repeat Rows 1 through 3.

Row 36: Repeat Row 32.

Armhole shaping

Row 37: K1, p across and using Knitted Cast-on, cast on 3 sts (arm edge).

Rows 38 and 39: Repeat Rows 2 and 3.

Row 40: K1, work Triple St 10 (11) times, k1.

Rows 41 through 43: Repeat Rows 37 through 39.

Row 44: K1, work Triple St 11 (12) times—35 (38) sts.

Rows 45 through 47: Repeat Rows 1 through 3.

Repeat Rows 44 through 47 for 7 (8) times more.

Ribbing

Row 1 (RS): K1, work Triple Rib St 11 (12) times, k1.

Row 2: P2, ★k1, p2; repeat from ★ across.

Row 3: K2, ★p1, k2.

Repeat Rows 2 and 3 once more. Bind off all sts in ribbing pattern. Cut yarn.

FINISHING

Sew side seams.

With right side of work facing you, crochet a row of single crochet up right front edge, around neckline, and down left front edge, spacing sts to keep edge smooth and flat.

Thread tapestry needle with 24"/61cm length of yarn. Thread yarn closure along front edges as though threading a shoelace (see Lace-up Closure on page 21). Securely fasten ends.

Weave in and trim all loose yarn ends.

This project was knit with 3 (4) skeins of Artyarns Supermerino, 100% Merino wool medium-weight yarn, 1.8oz/50g = 104yd/95m per skein, color #240 Eggplant.

Floating Stitch Tank

EXPERIENCE LEVEL
Intermediate

SIZES
Small (Medium, Large)

THIS VERSATILE CROPPED TANK CAN BE DRESSED UP FOR A GLITTERING NIGHT ON THE TOWN, OR DOWN FOR KICK-BACK COMFORT. WHEN MOHAIR IS ALTERNATED EVERY TWO ROWS, THE LACE STITCHES LOOK AS IF THEY ARE HANGING IN MID-AIR. IF CASHMERE IS SUBSTITUTED (SEE ALTERNATE VERSION ON PAGE 59), THE LOOK IS DIFFERENT, BUT JUST AS EXOTIC.

FINISHED MEASUREMENTS

Bust: 36 (38, 40)"/91.5 (96.5, 101.5)cm

Total length: 17 (17½, 18)"/43 (44.5, 45.5)cm

Standard fit, with 2"/5cm ease.

MATERIALS

Approx total: 163yd/149m silk lightweight yarn (yarn A), and

230yd/210m mohair and silk blend superfine yarn, or cashmere superfine yarn, (yarn B), and

50yd/46m ⅛"/3mm-wide silk ribbon (yarn C), optional for trim

Knitting needles: 4.5mm (size 7 U.S.) *or size to obtain gauge*

Crochet hook: 3.5mm (size E/4 U.S.)

Stitch holder

GAUGE

15 sts and 40 rows = 4"/10cm in Lace Pattern

Always take time to check your gauge.

PATTERN STITCH

Lace Pattern

(Multiple of 6 sts, plus 3)

Row 1 (WS): K3, *yarn over, slip 2 sts together as if to knit, k1, then pass both slipped sts over k st, yarn over, k3; repeat from * across.

Row 2 (RS): Purl across.

Repeat Rows 1 and 2 for pattern, alternating yarns A and B every 2 rows.

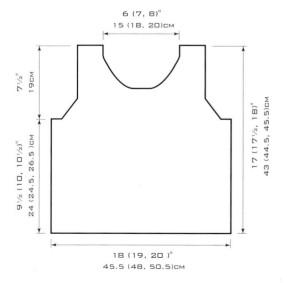

INSTRUCTIONS

BACK

With yarn A, cast on 65 (71, 77) sts.

Row 1: With A, k1 (selvage st), work Row 1 of Lace Pattern across to last st, k1 (selvage st).

Row 2: K1, work Row 2 of Lace Pattern across to last st, k1. Drop A and attach B.

Rows 3 and 4: With B, repeat rows 1 and 2. Drop B and pick up A.

Alternating A and B every 2 rows and carrying color not in use loosely along side edge of work, continue to repeat Rows 1 and 2 for Lace Pattern and maintain selvage st at each edge. Work until piece measures 9½ (10, 10½)"/24 (25.5, 26.5)cm from beginning.

Armhole shaping

Note: Maintain continuity of lace pattern throughout. When your shape armholes, for example, just knit across sts belonging to a lace pattern repeat on previous row if there are no longer 6 sts remaining. See Traveling Lace on page 8.

Bind off 4 sts at the beginning of next 2 rows, then 3 sts on next 2 rows, then 2 sts on next 2 rows. Dec 1 st at beginning and end of every other row twice.

Maintaining pattern, work even on remaining 43 (49, 55) sts until armholes measure 5 (5½, 6)"/12.5 (14, 15)cm.

Neck shaping

Next row: Keeping in pattern, work first 10 (11, 12) sts and place these sts on a holder, then bind off center 23 (27, 31) sts for back neck, then work remaining 10 (11, 12) sts.

Continue on these 10 (11, 12) sts until total armhole measures 7½"/19cm. Bind off these sts for shoulder.

Transfer the remaining 10 (11, 12) sts from holder onto needles, and complete to correspond to first shoulder.

FRONT

Work same as for Back until armholes measure 3½"/9cm—43 (49, 55) sts.

Neck shaping

Next row: Keeping in pattern, work first 10 (11, 12) sts and place these sts on a holder, then bind off center 23 (27, 31) sts for front neck, then work remaining 10 (11, 12) sts.

Continue on these 10 (11, 12) sts until total armhole measures 7½"/19cm. Bind off these sts for shoulder.

Transfer the remaining 10 (11, 12) sts from holder onto needles, and complete to correspond to first shoulder.

6 (7, 8)"
15 (18, 20)cm

7½"
19cm

9½ (10, 10½)"
24 (24.5, 26.5)cm

17 (17½, 18)"
43 (44.5, 45.5)cm

18 (19, 20)"
45.5 (48, 50.5)cm

FINISHING

With right sides together, using yarn B, seam shoulder, then side seams.

If desired, using yarn C and with right side of work facing you, crochet a row of single crochet (sc) all around neckline and around each armhole, spacing sts to keep edge smooth and flat.

Weave in yarn ends.

This project was knitted with 1 skein of Artyarns Regal Silk, 100% silk lightweight yarn, 1.8oz/50g = 163yd/149m per skein, color #248, brown (yarn A), and 1 skein of Artyarns Silk Mohair, 70% mohair/30% silk superfine yarn, .9oz/25g = 230yd/210m per skein, color #417, variegated beige (yarn B), and 1 skein of Artyarns Silk Ribbon, 100% silk ⅛"/3mm-wide ribbon, .9oz/25g = 138yd/126m per skein, color #248, brown (yarn C).

Alternate project was knit with 1 skein of Artyarns Regal Silk, 100% silk lightweight yarn, 1.8oz/50g = 163yd/149m per skein, color #246, black (yarn A), and 1 skein of Artyarns Cashmere 2 Ply, 100% cashmere superfine yarn, 1.8oz/50g = 255yd/233m per skein, color #246, black (yarn B), and 1 skein of Artyarns Silk Ribbon, 100% silk ⅛"/3mm-wide ribbon, .9oz/25g = 138yd/126m per skein, color #246, black (yarn C).

Baby's Breath Tee

EXPERIENCE LEVEL

Intermediate

SIZE

X-Small (Small, Medium, Large)

*Y*OU CAN'T HELP BUT FEEL EXCEEDINGLY FEMININE IN THIS HIP-SKIMMING TEE. THE LACE NECKLINE IS AS DELICATE AND LIGHT AS A SUMMER'S BREEZE. KNITTED IN TOGETHER WITH THE FRONT, THE NECKLINE USES A SILK MOHAIR YARN IN EXACTLY THE SAME COLOR AS THE SILK YARN USED FOR THE BODICE.

FINISHED MEASUREMENTS

Note: Measurements given below are for when this form-fitting garment is actually worn, and include several inches of stretching. The garment, lying flat and unstretched, will measure less than indicated below.

At bust: 32 (36, 40½, 45)"/81 (91.5, 103, 114.5)cm

Length to armhole: 14 (15, 15, 15½)"/35.5 (38, 38, 39.5)cm

Snug fit

MATERIALS

Approx total: 652 (815, 978, 1141)yd/546 (745, 894, 1043)m silk lightweight yarn (yarn A) and

230 (230, 230, 230)yd/210 (210, 210, 210)m mohair and silk blend superfine yarn (yarn B)

Circular needle: 4mm (size 6 U.S.) *or size to obtain gauge,* 24"/61cm long

Knitting needles (optional): 4mm (size 6 U.S.) *or size to obtain gauge*

GAUGE

19 sts and 24 rows = 4"/10cm in Lace Stitch pattern.

21 sts and 28 rows = 4"/10cm in St st

Always take time to check your gauge.

PATTERN STITCHES

St st in rounds

Knit every round.

St st in rows

Row 1 (RS): Knit.

Row 2: Purl.

Repeat these 2 rows of pattern.

Lace Pattern in rounds

(Multiple of 6 sts)

Round 1: K1, ★yo, k1, k3tog, k1, yo, k1; repeat from ★ to last 5 sts, yo, k1, k3tog, k1, yo.

Round 2: K1, ★p5, k1; repeat from ★ to last 5 sts, p5.

Repeat these 2 rounds for lace pattern.

Lace Pattern in rows

(Multiple of 6 sts, plus 2)

Row 1 (RS): K1, ★yo, k1, k3tog, k1, yo, k1; repeat from ★ to last st, k1.

Row 2: K1, ★p1, k5; repeat from ★ to last st, k1.

Repeat these 2 rows for lace pattern.

INSTRUCTIONS

LOWER BODY

Note: This piece is worked in rounds on a circular needle starting at the bottom and working upward to armholes.

With yarn A, cast on 156 (180, 204, 228) sts. Join work and mark beginning of rounds. Work Lace Pattern in rounds for 2¼"/5.5cm.

Waist shaping

Next row: K78 (90, 102, 114) sts, place marker on needle, k78 (90, 102, 114) sts. Beginning and center markers now indicate side "seams" of piece. Work 3 more rounds of St st.

Decrease Round: K1, k2tog, k to 3 sts before marker, SSK, k2, k2tog, k to last 3 sts before marker, SSK, k1, slipping each marker (4 sts decreased).

Continue in St st in rounds and repeat Decrease Round every fifth round 3 times more.

Work even in St st on remaining 140 (164, 188, 212) sts until piece measures 7½ (8, 8, 8½)"/19 (20, 20, 21.5)cm from beginning.

Increase Round: K2, M1, k to 2 sts before marker, M1, k4, M1, k to last 2 sts, M1, k2 (4 sts increased).

Continue in Stockinette St and repeat Increase Round every fifth round 3 times more.

Work even in St st on 156 (180, 204, 228) sts until piece measures 14 (15, 15, 15½)"/35.5 (38, 38, 39.5)cm from beginning.

Divide for armholes

Transfer the last completed 78 (90, 102, 114) sts between markers onto a holder for the front.

BACK

Change to straight needles if desired to work on back sts as follows:

Armhole shaping

Working St st in rows, bind off 6 sts at beginning of next 2 rows. Decrease 1 st at each end of every other row 3 times. Work even on remaining 60 (72, 84, 96) sts until armholes measure 7¾ (8, 8, 8¼)"/19.5 (20, 20, 21)cm, ending with a purl row.

Neck shaping

Next row: K12 (18, 24, 30) sts, attach another ball of yarn and with this new yarn, bind off center 36 sts. K remaining 12 (18, 24, 30) sts. Work each side separately with its own yarn and work as follows: At each neck edge decrease 1 st every row twice. At each arm edge, bind off remaining 10 (16, 22, 28) sts.

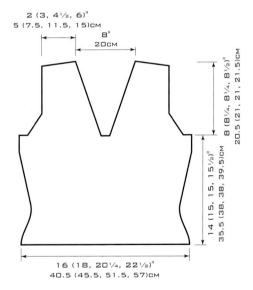

2 (3, 4½, 6)"
5 (7.5, 11.5, 15)cm

8"
20cm

8 (8¼, 8¼, 8½)"
20.5 (21, 21, 21.5)cm

14 (15, 15, 15½)"
35.5 (38, 38, 39.5)cm

16 (18, 20¼, 22½)"
40.5 (45.5, 51.5, 57)cm

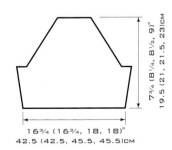

7¾ (8¼, 8½, 9)"
19.5 (21, 21.5, 23)cm

16¾ (16¾, 18, 18)"
42.5 (42.5, 45.5, 45.5)cm

FRONT

Transfer the 78 (90, 102, 112) front stitches from holder onto needle, using straight needles if desired. With right side of work facing you, join A at beginning of row.

Armhole shaping

Working St st in rows, bind off 6 sts at beginning of next 2 rows. Decrease 1 st at each end of next row, then every other row twice more; purl 1 row after last decrease row—60 (72, 84, 96) sts remain.

Neckline trim

Note: As you change from one yarn to the next yarn for working the trim section, be sure to wrap the yarns, bringing the new yarn up from under the previously used yarn to twist them and prevent holes in your work.

Row 1 (RS): With A, k26 (32, 38, 44) sts; drop A and attach B; with B, k8; drop B and attach a new ball of A; with new A, k remaining 26 (32, 38, 44) sts.

Work each section with its own separate yarn, remembering to twist yarns as you change from one to the next.

Row 2: With A, p25 (31, 37, 43); drop A and pick up B; with B, p10; drop B and pick up A; with A, p25 (31, 37, 43).

Row 3: With A, k24 (30, 36, 42); with B, k12; with A, k24 (30, 36, 42).

Row 4: With A, p23 (29, 35, 41); with B, p14; with A, p23 (29, 35, 41).

Row 5: With A, k22 (28, 34, 40); with B, k16; with A, k22 (28, 34, 40).

Row 6: With A, p21 (27, 33, 39); with B, p18; with A, p21 (27, 33, 39).

Row 7: With A, k20 (26, 32, 38); with B, k20; with A, k20 (26, 32, 38).

Row 8: With A, p19 (25, 31, 37); with B, p22; with A, p19 (25, 31, 37).

Row 9: With A, k18 (24, 30, 36); with B, k24; with A, k18 (24, 30, 36).

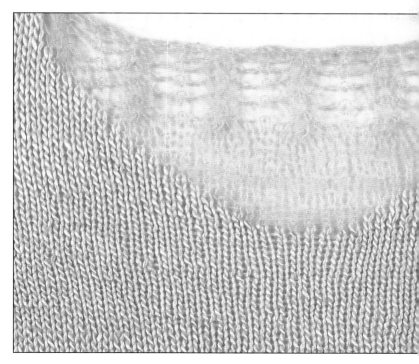

Row 10: With A, p17 (23, 29, 35); with B, p26; with A, p17 (23, 29, 35).

Row 11: With A, k16 (22, 28, 34); with B, k28; with A, k16 (22, 28, 34).

Row 12: With A, p15 (21, 27, 33); with B, p30; with A, p15 (21, 27, 33).

Row 13: With A, k 14 (20, 26, 32); with B, establish Lace Pattern in rows as follows:

K1, ★yo, k1, k3tog, k1, yo, k 1; repeat from ★ 4 times more, k1; with A, k14 (20, 26, 32).

Row 14: With A, p13 (19, 25, 31); with B, k2, ★ p1, k5; repeat from ★ 4 times more, p1, k1; with A, p13 (19, 25, 31).

Row 15: With A, k12 (18, 24, 30); with B, k3,★yo, k1, k3tog, k1, yo, k1; repeat from ★ 4 times more, k3; with A, k12 (18, 25, 30).

Row 16: With A, p11 (17, 23, 29); with B, k4, ★p1, k5; repeat from ★ 4 times, p1, k3; with A, p11 (17, 23, 29).

Row 17: With A, k10 (16, 22, 28); with B, k4 [k1, yo, k1, k3tog, k1, yo] 5 times, k6; with A, k10 (16, 22, 28).

Row 18: With A, p10 (16, 22, 28); with B, ★p5, k1; repeat from ★ 5 times more, p4; with A, p10 (16, 22, 28).

Rows 19 through 22: Repeat Rows 17 and 18 twice more.

Row 23: With A, k10 (16, 22, 28); with B, loosely bind off all 40 sts of trim section; with A, k10 (16, 22, 28).

Shoulders

Work each side separately with its own ball of A, continuing in St st until armholes measure 8 (8¼, 8¼, 8½)"/20.5 (21, 21, 21.5)cm. Bind off all remaining sts on each side.

SLEEVES

Make 2.

With yarn A and straight needles if desired, cast on 80 (80, 86, 86) sts. Work in Lace Pattern in rows for 12 rows.

Cap shaping

Working in St st in rows for remainder of sleeve, bind off 6 sts at beginning of next 2 rows. Decrease 1 st at each end of every other row 3 times—62 (62, 68, 68) sts.

Work even for 4 rows. Then decrease 1 st at each end of every row 8 (2, 6, 4) times, then decrease 1 st at each end every other row 7 (12, 11, 13) times—32 (34, 34, 34) sts. Bind off 3 (4, 4, 4) sts at beginning of next 2 rows, then bind off 2 sts at beginning of next 4 rows. Bind off remaining sts.

FINISHING

With right sides together, sew front to back along shoulder seams. Sew underarm seam of each sleeve. With right sides together, pin a sleeve to one arm-hole, matching center top of cap to shoulder seam and sleeve seam to center of body armhole; sew sleeve in place. Repeat for other sleeve.

BONUS PROJECT

WANT MORE USING THIS TECHNIQUE?
VISIT WWW.ARTYARNS.COM

With crochet hook and yarn A, work a row of single crochet (sc) around neck edge, omitting neckline trim section on front and spacing sts to keep edge smooth and flat.

Weave in yarn ends.

This project was knit with 4 (5, 6, 7) skeins of Artyarns Regal Silk, 100% silk lightweight yarn, 1.8oz/50g = 163yd/149m per skein, color #223, pale yellow (yarn A), and

1 skein Artyarns Silk Mohair, 70% mohair/ 30% silk blend superfine yarn, 9oz/25g =230yd/210m per skein, color #223, pale yellow (yarn B).

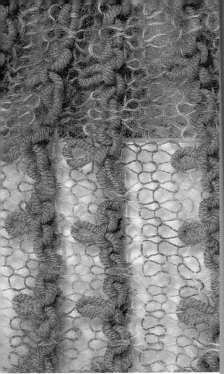

Gwenivere's Choice Tunic

EXPERIENCE LEVEL

Intermediate

SIZE

Small (Medium, Large, X-Large)

With its filmy, flowing sleeves, and fitted bodice, this tunic could very well have come straight from the chivalrous days of King Arthur. The shapely bodice gives way to gauzy stitches that appear to be suspended in thin air, thanks to an easy, drop-stitch pattern.

Finished Measurements

Bust: About 32 (35, 39, 42)"/81 (89, 99, 106.5)cm

Bottom Edge: 43½ (48, 52½, 57)"/110.5 (122, 133.5, 145)cm

Length to armhole: 17 (17½, 18, 18½)"/43 (44.5, 45.5, 47)cm

Total length: 25 (26, 27, 28)"/63.5 (66, 68.5, 71)cm

Materials

Approx total: 564 (752, 752, 940)yd/516 (688, 688, 860)m Merino wool medium-weight yarn (yarn A), and

690 (920, 920, 920)yd/630 (840, 840, 840)m mohair/silk blend superfine yarn (yarn B)

Scrap yarn for provisional casting-on and holding stitches

Knitting needles: 5mm (size 8 U.S.) *or size to maintain gauge*, and same-size extra needle for 3-needle binding off

2 stitch holders

Tapestry needle

Gauge

18 sts and 40 rows = 4"/10cm in Slip Stitch Pattern 4

Always take time to check your gauge.

Pattern Stitches

Slip Stitch Pattern 1

(Multiple of 4 sts, plus 3)

Row 1 (RS): With yarn A, ★k3, sl 1 wyib; repeat from ★ across to last 3 sts, k3.

Row 2: With A, ★k3, sl 1 wyif; repeat from ★ across to last 3 sts, k3.

Row 3: With B, k1, ★sl 1 wyib, k3; repeat from ★ across to last 2 sts, sl 1 wyib, k1.

Row 4: With B, k1, ★sl 1 wyif, k3; repeat from ★ across to last 2 sts, sl 1 wyif, k1.

Row 5: With B, knit across.

Row 6: With B, k1, purl across to last st, k1.

Slip Stitch Pattern 2, with short rows

(Multiple of 4 sts, plus 3)

Note: See Wrapping Short Rows on page 15. Each time you repeat this pattern, you will purl a *different number of stitches* on Row 6 for the short rows, as indicated below.

Row 1 (RS): With A, ★k3, sl 1 wyib; repeat from ★ across to last 3 sts, k3.

Row 2: With A, ★k3, sl 1 wyif; repeat from ★ across to last 3 sts, k3.

Row 3: With B, k1, ★sl 1 wyib, k3; repeat from ★ across to last 2 sts, sl 1 wyib, k1.

Row 4: With B, k1, ★sl 1 wyif, k3; repeat from ★ across to last 2 sts, sl 1 wyif, k1.

Row 5: With B, k across.

Row 6 (short row): With B, p26 (on the first time you work this row), wrap, turn; k to end; turn work and p across all sts to end, picking up wrap. The next time you repeat this pattern row, p22, the following time, p18 sts, then p26 sts as you work across Row 6, to repeat the sequence.

Slip Stitch Pattern 3, with short rows

(Multiple of 4 sts, plus 3)

Note: See Wrapping Short Rows on page 15. Each time you repeat this pattern, you will knit a *different number of stitches* on Row 5 for the short rows, as indicated below.

Row 1 (RS): With A, ★k3, sl 1 wyib; repeat from ★ across to last 3 sts, k3.

Row 2: With A, ★k3, sl 1 wyif; repeat from ★ across to last 3 sts, k3.

Row 3: With B, k1, ★sl 1 wyib, k3; repeat from ★ across to last 2 sts, sl 1 wyib, k1.

Row 4: With B, k1, ★sl 1 wyif, k3; repeat from ★ across to last 2 sts, sl 1 wyif, k1.

Row 5 (short row): With B, k26 (on first time you work this row), wrap, turn; p to end; turn and k across all sts to end, picking up wrap. The next time you repeat this row, k22 sts, the following time 18, then 26 sts as you work across Row 5, to repeat the sequence.

Row 6: With B, p across.

Slip Stitch Pattern 4

(Multiple of 4 sts, plus 3)

Row 1 (RS): With yarn A, ★k3, sl 1 wyib; repeat from ★ across to last 3 sts, k3.

Row 2: With A, ★k3, sl 1 wyif; repeat from ★ across to last 3 sts, k3.

Row 3: With B, k1, ★ sl 1 wyib, k3; repeat from ★ across to last 2 sts, sl 1 wyib, k1.

Row 4: With B, k1, ★ sl 1 wyif, k3; repeat from ★ across to last 2 sts, sl 1 wyif, k1.

INSTRUCTIONS

LOWER BODY SECTION

Note: To keep the stitch pattern symmetrical, the lower body section is knitted in two panels, each worked side to side, beginning at center front and worked to center back where the two panels are joined together. Worked sideways, the pattern forms vertical lines. Short rows are used to shape the panels and provide the A-line fullness at the bottom edge.

Right side panel

With A, cast on 55 (59, 63, 67, 71) sts.

Work the 6 rows of Slip Stitch Pattern 1, followed by the 6 rows of Slip Stitch Pattern 2. Continue to alternate these 2 patterns for a total of 9 (10, 11, 12) times, then work Slip Stitch Pattern 1 once more. Place all stitches on a stitch holder. Cut yarn.

Left side panel

With A, cast on 55 (59, 63, 67, 71) sts.

Work the 6 rows of Slip Stitch Pattern 1, followed by the 6 rows of Slip Stitch Pattern 3, alternating these 2 patterns for a total of 9 (10, 11, 12) times, then work Slip Stitch Pattern 1 once more, leaving sts on needle and B attached.

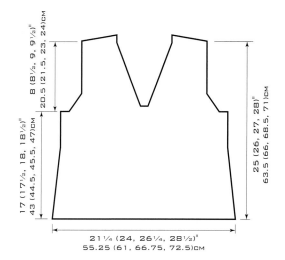

Joining panels

Transfer right side panel sts to second needle. With right sides of panels together and wrong side facing out, and using third needle and B, work 3-needle bind-off method (see page 20) to join the panels. Cut yarn.

BODICE

With yarn A and right side of work facing you, pick up and k 143 (155, 175, 187) sts evenly spaced across top edge of lower section.

Work Slip Stitch Pattern 4 for 4"/10cm, ending with a wrong side row.

Armhole and neck shaping

Keeping continuity of Slip Stitch Pattern 4 as established, work first 33 (36, 41, 44) sts and place these sts on a stitch holder for right front, bind off 6 sts for armhole, work next 65 (71, 81, 87) sts, and place these sts on another stitch holder for back. Bind off 6 sts for armhole, work remaining 33 (36, 41, 44) sts for left front.

Continue working on left front sts only as follows:

Left front

Keeping pattern as established, at front neck edge bind off 1 st every row 12 times and at the same time, at arm edge, bind off 2 sts once, then at same edge decrease 1 st every other row twice—17 (20, 25, 28) sts remain after all shaping is completed.

Work even in pattern until armhole measures 8 (8½, 9, 9½)"/20 (21.5, 23, 24)cm. Bind off all sts.

Right front

Transfer right front sts from holder to needle. Attach yarn at front edge (neck edge), and work to correspond to left front.

Back

Transfer back sts from holder to needle. Attach yarn and working in pattern as established, bind off 2 sts at beginning of next 4 rows, then decrease 1 st at each end every other row 2 (2, 3, 3) times—53 (59, 67, 73) sts. Work even in pattern until armholes measure same as for fronts. Bind off all sts for shoulders and back neck.

SLEEVES

Note: For symmetry, lower portion of one sleeve is knitted sideways in one direction and on the other sleeve, in the opposite direction, in vertical rows.

Left sleeve

With A and piece of scrap yarn, using provisional cast-on method (see page 19), cast on 43 (47, 51, 55) sts. Alternate Slip Stitch Pattern 1 and Slip Stitch Pattern 2 for a total of 6 (7, 8, 9) times, then work the 6 rows of Slip Stitch Pattern 1 once more.

Thread tapestry needle with 1yd/.9m length of scrap yarn and thread needle through sleeve sts (to make a flexible stitch holder), and tie ends of scrap yarn together to hold sts in place.

Rotate piece so narrow edge (opposite short rows) is at top, with cast-on edge and holder sts at sides. With A, pick up and knit 51 (55, 55, 59) sts evenly spaced across top edge of the sleeve piece.

Work in Slip Stitch Pattern 4 and, keeping continuity of pattern as established, increase 1 st at each end of every 6th row 8 (6, 8, 2) times, then every 8th row 1 (3, 2, 7) times—69 (73, 75, 77) sts.

Cap shaping

Bind off 3 sts at beginning of next 2 rows, then bind off 2 sts at beginning of next 4 rows.

Decrease 1 st each end every other row 10 (13, 11, 10) times, then every 4th row 3 (2, 4, 5) times. Work even if needed until cap measures 4½ (4¾, 5¼, 5½)"/11.5 (12, 13.5, 14)cm. Bind off 2 sts at beginning of next 4 rows, then bind off 3 (3, 4, 4) sts at beginning of next 2 rows. Bind off all remaining sts.

Right Sleeve

Work to correspond to left sleeve, alternating Slip Stitch Pattern 1 with Slip Stitch Pattern 3.

FINISHING

Block all pieces to measurements.

On one sleeve, remove scrap yarn from provisional cast-on sts and place them on a needle. Transfer sts from yarn holder to another needle. With right sides together, using extra needle, work 3-needle bind-off method (see page 20) to seam piece. Then seam together edges of upper sleeve section. Repeat for second sleeve.

With right sides of back and fronts together, sew shoulder seams. Sew a sleeve cap to each armhole, matching center top of sleeve to shoulder seam and sleeve seam centered on bound-off sts of underarm.

Cut a length of yarn A about 60"/152.5cm. To lace front edges together, start at bottom and work upward, working through the eyelets along front edge to lace as if you were threading a shoelace, crossing back and forth between fronts to the neck edge. Tie ends in a bow at top, and cut off excess yarn ends.

This project was knit with 3 (4, 4, 5) skeins of Artyarns Ultramerino 8, 100% Merino wool medium-weight yarn, 3½oz/100g = 188yd/172m per skein, color #201, rust orange (yarn A), and

3 (4, 4, 4) skeins of Artyarns Silk Mohair, 70% kid mohair/30% silk blend superfine yarn, .9oz/25g = 230yd/210m per skein, color #136, variegated colors (yarn B).

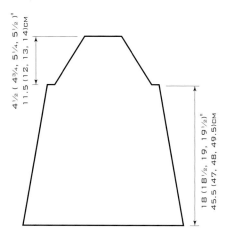

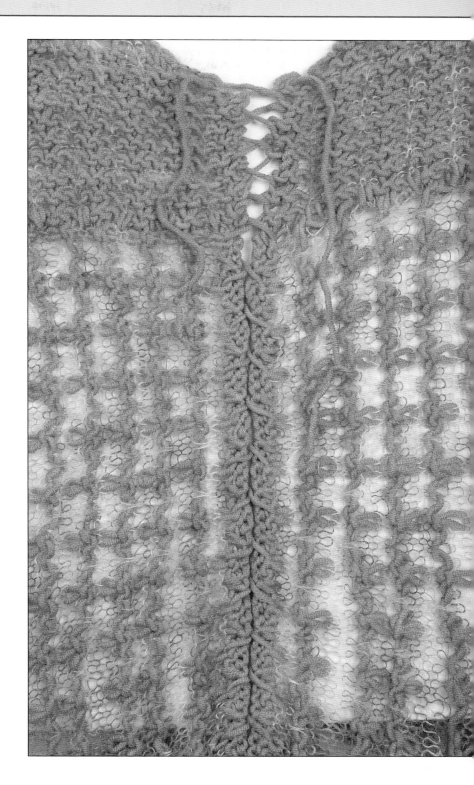

MODULAR LACE PART 1:

CHEVRONS,
DIAGONAL TRIANGLES
AND SQUARES

The projects in this chapter combine lace and diagonal knitting in an unusual way. Knitted chevrons, triangles, and squares are sometimes angled, sometimes turned on end to form dazzling patterns within patterns, making for unexpected visual treats.

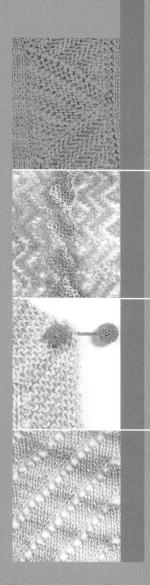

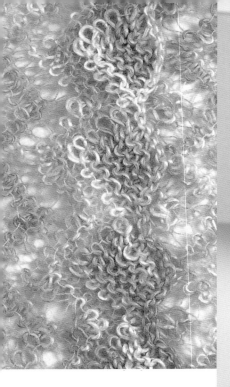

Sheer Bliss Halter

■

EXPERIENCE LEVEL

Intermediate

SIZES

Petite (X-Small, Small, Medium,
Large, X-Large)

DARING SQUIGGLES KNITTED SIDE-TO-SIDE ZIGZAG PLAYFULLY UP AND DOWN THIS SHOWY HALTER. AN ATTACHED BEADED NECKLACE ELIMINATES THE NEED FOR ANY JEWELRY. DOUBLE-TAKES GUARANTEED.

FINISHED MEASUREMENTS

Bust: 30 (32, 34, 36, 38, 42)"/76 (81, 86.5, 91.5, 96.5, 106.5)cm

Length: 12½"/32cm

Snug fit (use actual bust measurement with little or no ease to determine desired size).

MATERIALS

Approx total: 260yd/238m silk and silk/mohair blend medium-weight 2-strand yarn (yarn A), and 100yd/91m mohair and silk blend superfine weight yarn in *each of 3 different colors* to coordinate with yarn A (yarns B, C, and D), 50yd/45m ⅛"/3mm-wide silk ribbon for optional trim (yarn E)

Circular needles: 4.5mm (size 7 U.S.) *or size to obtain gauge*, 24"/61cm long

Crochet hook: 3.25mm (size D/3 U.S.)

Stitch marker

Stitch holder

4mm round turquoise beads, about 110, or enough to make a 21 to 23"/53.5 to 58.5cm strand

Flexible beading wire

1"/2.5cm silver clasp

GAUGE

16 sts and 32 rows = 4"/10cm in Garter Stitch

Always take time to check your gauge.

PATTERN STITCHES

Garter Stitch

Knit every row.

Long Stitch

Knit each stitch wrapping yarn two times around needle to form 2 loops. On following row knit into first loop and drop second loop to form elongated stitch.

Chevron Pattern

(Multiple of 10 sts)

Row 1: *K4, inc 1, k3, k2tog; repeat from * to end.

Row 2: K4, inc 1, *k4, k2tog, k3, inc 1; repeat from * to last 5 sts, k3, k2tog.

Long St Chevron Pattern

Row 1: K1, work long st in each of next 3 sts, inc 1, Long st in each of next 3 sts, k2tog, *Long st in each of next 4 sts, inc 1, Long st in each of next 3 sts, k2tog; repeat from * across.

Row 2: Knitting into only first wrap of double-wrapped Long sts and dropping second wrap, k4, inc 1, *k4, k2tog, k3, inc 1; repeat from * to last 5 sts, k3, k2tog.

Chevron Pattern in the Round

Round 1: *K4, inc 1, k3, k2tog; repeat from * around.

Round 2: *P4, inc 1 (purl), p3, p2tog; repeat from * around.

Repeat these 2 rounds for Chevron Pattern in the round.

INSTRUCTIONS

HALTER

Note: This halter is knitted from side to side and is worked in three steps: overlapping front border, the body, then the decorative bottom panel worked separately and sewn to the lower edge.

STEP 1: FRONT BORDER

With yarn A, cast on 60 sts. Work back and forth in rows on circular needle. Work 6 diagonal diamonds for front border as follows:

Row 1: Inc 1, k3, k2tog, turn; sl 1, k4, turn, leaving 1 st unworked.

Row 2: Inc 1, k3, k2tog, turn; sl 1, k4, turn, leaving 2 sts unworked.

Rows 3 and 4: Continue to work as for Row 1, leaving 1 additional st unworked on each following row—4 sts left unworked at end of Row 4.

Row 5: Inc 1, k3, k2tog, do not turn—10 worked sts.

Repeat Rows 1 through 5 for 5 more times until all the original 60 cast-on sts have been used. Drop A and attach B.

STEP 2: BODY

Continuing on Step 1 sts, work body section as follows:

Note: From now on, interchange yarns A, B, C, and D every 2 rows as indicated, carrying A and any other uncut color not in use loosely alongside edge of work.

Rows 1 and 2: With B, work Chevron Pattern. Drop B and pick up A.

Rows 3 and 4: With A, work Chevron Pattern.

Rows 5 and 6: With B, work Long St Chevron Pattern. Cut B.

Rows 7 and 8: With A, work Chevron Pattern. Attach C.

Rows 9 and 10: With C, work Chevron Pattern.

Rows 11 and 12: With A, work Chevron Pattern.

Rows 13 and 14: With C, work Long St Chevron Pattern. Cut C.

Rows 15 and 16: With A, work Chevron Pattern. Attach D.

Rows 17 and 18: With D, work Chevron Pattern.

Rows 19 and 20: With A, work Chevron Pattern.

Rows 21 and 22: With D, work Long St Chevron Pattern. Cut D.

Repeat Rows 1 through 22 for pattern until the Step 2 section of the piece measures the desired size (do not include overlapping Step 1 section in your measurement).

Bind off all sts. Cut yarn.

STEP 3: BOTTOM PANEL

With A, cast onto circular needle 160 (170, 180, 190, 200, 210) sts for decorative bottom panel. Join sts and work in rounds as follows:

Rounds 1 through 10: Work in Chevron Pattern in the Round, working 2 rows each of A, B, C, D, and A.

Bind off all sts loosely. Cut yarn and weave in yarn ends.

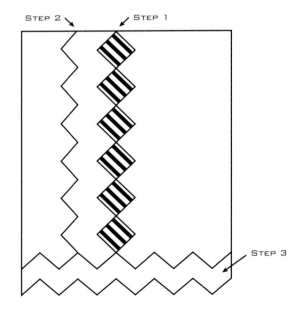

FINISHING

Attach ends of halter top to form a tube as follows: With Step 1 diamonds overlapping bound-off sts, pin these overlapping edges together. Working from the wrong side, neatly sew the edges together with yarn B for an invisible seam. The diamond border forms the center front of the halter on the right side of the piece. Match the center of the Step 3 border to the vertical center of the diamond border; and with the top half of the border covering the bottom edge of the halter (and the lower half extending below the halter bottom), seam the bottom border neatly in place.

Crochet a row of single crochet (sc) around the halter top, using yarn E.

Necklace

Attach one half of silver clasp to one end of wire length. For finished necklace with a length of 21 to 23"/53.5 to 58.5cm, string 10 to 11"/25.5 to 28cm length of beads onto wire. Then thread beading wire securely into top of diamond at center front neck edge. Then string an equal length of beads onto remaining wire, and secure the second half of the clasp in place. Cut wire and weave in ends.

The project was knit with 1 skein of Artyarns Silk Rhapsody, 100% silk and 70% mohair/30% silk blend, medium-weight 2-strand yarn, 3½oz/100g = 260yd/238m per skein, color #2204, variegated turquoise (yarn A), and

1 skein Artyarns Silk Mohair, 70% mohair/30% silk blend, superfine yarn, .9oz/25g = 230yd/210m per skein, color #414, variegated turquoise (yarn B), and

1 skein Artyarns Silk Mohair, 70% mohair/30% silk blend, superfine yarn, .9oz/25g = 230yd/210m per skein, color #412, variegated green (yarn C), and

1 skein Artyarns Silk Mohair, 70% mohair/30% silk blend, superfine yarn, .9oz/25g = 230yd/210m per skein, color #416, variegated purple (yarn D), and

1 skein Artyarns Silk Ribbon, 100% silk, ⅛"/3mm-wide ribbon, .9oz/25g = 138yd/126m per skein, color #204, turquoise (yarn E).

BONUS PROJECT

WANT MORE USING THIS TECHNIQUE?
VISIT WWW.ARTYARNS.COM

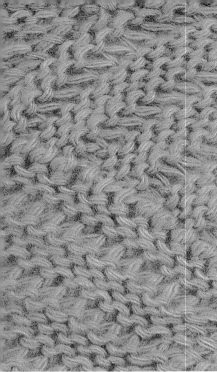

Multi Directional Sweater

EXPERIENCE LEVEL
Intermediate

SIZES
X-Small (Small, Medium, Large)

T HE UNUSUAL CONSTRUCTION AND BREEZY LACY SLEEVES WILL MAKE THIS SPECIAL PIECE STAND OUT IN ANY CROWD. THE TRIANGULAR BAND IS KNIT RIGHT INTO THE STOCKINETTE STITCH FABRIC, KEEPING THE KNITTING INTERESTING.

FINISHED MEASUREMENTS

Bust: 31 (34, 37, 40)"/79 (86, 94, 101.5)cm

Length, excluding bottom trim: 15½ (19½, 21¼, 22½)"/39 (49.5, 54, 57)cm

MATERIALS

Approx totals: 510 (612, 714, 714)yd/466 (558, 651, 651)m cashmere medium-weight yarn

Knitting needles: 5mm (size 8 U.S.), *or size needed to obtain gauge*

Circular needle: 5mm (size 8 U.S.), *or size needed to obtain gauge*, 16"/40.5cm long

3 clip-on stitch markers

Stitch holders

Crochet hook for finishing: 3.25mm (size D/3 U.S.)

Tapestry needle

GAUGE

16 sts and 25 rows = 4"/10cm in Stockinette st

Always take time to check your gauge.

STITCH GLOSSARY

Stockinette st: knit on right side rows, purl on wrong side rows.

Long st: Knit long st by wrapping yarn around needle twice (instead of once) and drawing both loops through stitch. On following row, work into just the first loop of each st, dropping second loop from needle to form the elongated st. Long st is not worked in any increased or decreased stitches.

Note 1: Both front and back pieces are worked in three continuous sections: The two outer sections are worked in Stockinette Stitch and the center panel is worked over the center 9 (10, 11, 12) cast-on stitches, working the Triangle 1 Pattern first, then repeating the Triangle 2 Pattern.

Markers #1 and #2 separate this center panel from the outer Stockinette Stitch sections.

TRIANGLE 1 PATTERN

Row 1: Inc 1, k1, turn; sl 1, k2.

Row 2: Inc 1, k3, turn; sl 1, k4.

Row 3: Inc 1, k5, turn; sl 1, k6.

Row 4: Inc 1, work 7 Long sts, turn; dropping extra wraps, sl 1, k8.

Row 5: Inc 1, k9, turn; sl 1, k10.

Row 6: Inc 1, k11, turn; sl 1, k12.

Row 7: Inc 1, work 13 Long sts, turn; dropping extra wraps, sl 1, k14.

For X-Small size only, work:

Row 8: Inc 1, k15. Triangle 1 completed.

For all other sizes, work:

Row 8: Inc 1, k15, turn; sl 1, k16.

For Small size only, work:

Row 9: Inc 1, k17. Triangle 1 completed.

For Medium and Large sizes only:

Row 9: Inc 1, k17, turn; sl 1, k18.

For Medium size only, work:

Row 10: Inc 1, k 19. Triangle 1 completed.

For Large size only, work:

Row 10: Inc 1, k19, turn; sl 1, k20.

Row 11: Inc 1, k21. Triangle 1 completed.

TRIANGLE 2 PATTERN

Row 1: Inc 1, SSK, turn; sl 1, k to end of panel.

Row 2: Inc 1, k1, SSK, turn; k to end.

Row 3: Inc 1, k2, SSK, turn; sl 1, k to end.

Row 4: Inc 1, work 3 Long sts, SSK, turn; dropping extra wraps, sl 1, k to end.

Row 5: Inc 1, k4, SSK, turn; sl 1, k to end.

Row 6: Inc 1, k5, SSK, turn; sl 1, k to end.

Row 7: Inc 1, work 6 Long sts, SSK, turn; dropping extra wraps, sl 1, k to end.

Row 8: Inc 1, k7, SSK, turn; sl 1, k to end.

Row 9: Inc 1, k8, SSK, turn; sl 1, k to end.

Row 10: Inc 1, work 9 Long sts, SSK, turn; dropping extra wraps, sl 1, k to end.

Row 11: Inc 1, k10, SSK, turn; sl 1, k to end.

Row 12: Inc 1, k11, SSK, turn; sl 1, k to end.

Row 13: Inc 1, work 12 Long sts, SSK, turn; dropping extra wraps, sl 1, k to end.

Row 14: Inc 1, k13, SSK, turn; sl 1, k to end.

For X-Small size only, work:

Row 15: Inc 1, k14, SSK. Triangle 2 completed.

For all other sizes, work:

Row 15: Inc 1, k14, SSK, turn; sl 1, k to end.

Row 16: Incl 1, work 15 Long sts, SSK, turn; dropping extra wraps, sl 1, k to end.

For Small size only:

Row 17: Inc 1, k 16, SSK. Triangle 2 completed.

For Medium and Large sizes only, work:

Row 17: Inc 1, k16, SSK, turn; sl 1, k to end.

Row 18: Inc 1, k 17, SSK, turn; sl 1, k to end.

For Medium size only, work:

Row 19: Inc 1, k18, SSK. Triangle 2 completed.

For Large size only, work:

Row 19: Inc 1, work 18 Long sts, SSK, turn; dropping extra wraps, sl 1, k to end.

Row 20: Inc 1, k19, SSK, turn; sl 1, k to end.

Row 21: Inc 1, k20, SSK. Triangle 2 completed.

Note 2: Most of the instruction rows consist of two partial rows, one knitting toward the center panel and working the center panel, then working back to the edge over the same stitches just worked.

Instructions

Back

Using straight or circular needles, cast on 61 (68, 75, 82) sts.

Step 1: Triangle 1 Section RS

Note: Each row begins on the RS and ends on the WS, until the last row.

Row 1: K26 (29, 32, 35), PM#1, work Row 1 of Base Triangle, slip marker, p25 (28, 31, 34), k1.

Rows 2 through 7 (8, 9, 10): K to marker #1, slip marker, work corresponding row of Triangle 1 (that is, on Row 2, work Row 2 of Triangle 1; on Row 3, work Row 3 of Triangle 1, and so on), slip marker, p back to last st, k1. Work until 7 (8, 9, 10) rows of Triangle 1 are completed.

Next row (RS): K to marker #1, slip marker, work Row 8 (9, 10, 11) of Triangle 1, PM#2, continuing RS row, k 26 (29, 32, 35), ending at opposite edge.

Step 2: Triangle 2 Section WS

Note: Each row begins on WS and ends on RS, until the last row.

Rows 1 through 14 (16, 18, 20): K1, p to marker #2, work corresponding row of Triangle 2 (that is, on Row 1, work Row 1 of Triangle 2; on Row 2, work Row 2 of Triangle 2, and so on), slip marker #2, k back to edge. Work until 14 (16, 18, 20) rows of Triangle 2 are completed.

Next row (WS): K1, p to marker #2, slip marker, work Row 15 (17, 19, 21) of Triangle 2, slip marker #1, continuing across WS row, p25 (28, 31, 34), k1, ending at opposite edge.

STEP 3: TRIANGLE 2 SECTION RS

Note: Each row begins on RS and ends on WS, until last row.

Rows 1 through 14 (16, 18, 20): K to marker #1, slip marker, work corresponding row of Triangle 2, slip marker #1, p back to the last st, k1. Work until 14 (16, 18, 20) rows of Triangle 2 are completed.

Next row (RS): K to marker #1, work Row 15 (17, 19, 21) of Triangle 2, slip marker #2, k26 (29, 32, 35), ending at opposite edge.

Repeat Step 2 once more. Repeat Step 3 and at the same time, when Row 7 (8, 9, 10) is completed, shape right armhole as follows:

Armhole shaping

At arm edge, bind off 4 sts once, then 3 sts once, then 1 st 3 times. Work even on remaining sts in established pattern, to complete Step 3. Now repeat Step 2 and work left armhole to correspond to right armhole.

When Step 2 is completed, repeat Step 3 until Row 8 (10, 12, 14) of Triangle 2 is completed, ending at arm edge.

Right shoulder shaping

Row 1: Bind off all 16 (19, 22, 25) sts to marker #1, RM, bind off next st, transfer stitch back to left needle.

Row 2: Continuing across triangle, SKP, k7 (9, 11, 13), SSK, turn; PM#1, k to end.

Row 3: SKP, k to marker #1, RM, SSK, turn; sl 1, PM #1, k to end.

Repeat Row 3, adding a Long st row every 3 ridges (6 rows), and ending with SKP, k3 (5, 7, 9), RM, SSK. K to opposite edge, slipping marker 2.

Left shoulder shaping

Row 1: K1, p to marker #2, slip marker #2, inc 1, SSK, turn; sl 1, PM #1, k to marker #2, slip marker, k to end.

Row 2: K1, p to marker #2, slip marker #2, inc 1, k to marker #1, RM#1, SSK, turn; sl 1, PM #1, k to marker #2, slip marker #2, k to end.

Repeat Row 2 for 0 (1, 2, 3) times more.

Next row: K1, p to marker #2, slip marker #2, SKP, k to marker #1, RM#1, SSK, turn; sl 1, PM#1, k to marker #2, slip marker #2, k to end.

Repeat this row 0 (1, 2, 3) times more.

Last row: K1, p to marker #2, RM#2, SKP, k to marker #1, RM#1, SSK, turn; bind off all remaining sts.

FRONT

Work same as for back, shaping armholes, until on the last repeat of Step 2 Rows 1 to 6 (7, 8, 9) is completed, ending as follows:

K1, p to marker #2, slip marker, work Row 7 (8, 9, 10) of Triangle 2, place all the sts between markers #1 and #2 on a stitch holder for center-front neck edge, removing the markers; continuing across WS row, p to last st, k1, ending at opposite edge.

Neck edge shaping

Work each side separately. Continuing on left side of front, work in Stockinette St and at neck edge, decrease 1 st every other row until 10 (12, 14, 15) sts remain on this side. Work even until armhole measures same as for back to shoulder. Bind off all sts on this side. Cut yarn and attach to right side at neck edge and work to correspond to left side.

SLEEVES

Make 2.

Note: Sleeve is worked in 4 steps, beginning at top of cap with a center-increase triangle, cap shaping, then each side is worked separately.

Step 1: Cap top with center-increase triangle

Cast on 3 sts.

Row 1: K1, inc 1, PM, k1, turn – 4 sts.

Row 2: Inc 1, RM, inc 1, PM, k2 – 6 sts.

Row 3: Inc 1, k to marker, RM, inc 1, PM, k to end.

Repeat Row 3, inserting Long st Row every 6th row, until there are 20 (20, 22, 24) sts on needle.

Step 2: Cap shaping

Row 1: K to marker, RM, inc 1, PM, k to end.

Repeat Row 1 until there are 46 (48, 50, 52) sts on needle.

Step 3: First side

Separate the sts, placing the half farthest from the working yarn onto a stitch holder. Work the remaining 23 (24, 25, 26) sts as follows:

Row 1: K to last st, sl 1, turn; SKP, k to end.

Repeat Row 1 until 14 (16, 18, 20) sts remain on needle.

Now square off edge as follows:

Row 1: K to last st, sl 1, turn; SKP, k to last 2 sts, k2tog.

Repeat this last row until 2 sts remain on needle. Bind off both sts.

Step 4: Second side

Place sts from holder onto needle. Attach yarn to top of triangle, and work as follows: SKP, k to end.

Repeat Step 3.

FINISHING

Block pieces.

With right sides of front and back together, seam shoulders and side edges. Seam underarm seam of each sleeve. Right sides of work together, sew a sleeve to each armhole, matching underarm seams and center top of sleeve cap to shoulder seam.

Neckline

Transfer center panel stitches from stitch holder to knitting needle. With crochet hook, starting at shoulder seam, single crochet around front half of neckline, single crochet into center panel stitches on knitting needle, and single crochet around remaining neckline. Cut yarn.

Weave in all yarn ends.

Bottom border

Border is worked in 5 steps.

With right side facing, starting at right side seam, pick up 1 stitch in the center of side seam, then 60 (66, 74, 80) along front side, then 1 stitch in the center of next side seam, then 60 (66, 74, 80) along back side--122 (134, 150, 162) stitches. Clip on 1 marker between stitch 30 (33, 37, 40) and 31 (34, 38, 41) of front, and a second marker between stitch 30 (33, 37, 40) and 31 (34, 38, 41) of back.

STEP 1: RIGHT SIDE BORDER

Begin Center Increase triangle in next stitch (center of right side seam) as follows:

Row 1: Inc 1, k2, turn; sl 1, k1, inc 1, k2, turn.

Row 2: Sl 1, k1, inc 1, k4, turn; sl 1, k3, inc 1, k4, turn.

Row 3: Sl 1, k3, inc1, k6, turn; sl 1, k5, inc 1, k6, turn.

Row 4: Sl 1, k5, inc1, k8, turn; sl 1, k7, inc 1, k8, turn.

Row 5: Sl 1, work 7 Long sts, inc 1, work 10 Long sts, turn; dropping extra wraps, sl 1, k9, inc 1, k10.

STEP 2: SEPARATE TRIANGLE SIDES

Work triangle stitches separately as follows: Transfer 11 triangle stitches farthest from working yarn onto stitch holder, and turn and k11 (top of triangle). Work one side at a time as follows:

Row 1: SKP, k10, turn; k to end.

Repeat Row 1, inserting a Long st row every 4th row, until you have reached center of back as indicated by marker. Place 11 stitches on holder, and cut yarn.

Transfer stitches from holder on other side of right side seam to needles. Attach yarn at top.

Row 1: SKP, k10, turn; k to end.

Repeat Row 1, inserting a Long st row every 4th row, until you have reached center of front as indicated by marker. Place 11 stitches on holder, and cut yarn.

STEP 3: LEFT SIDE BORDER

Attach yarn to left side seam, and repeat Steps 1 to 2, working to correspond to right side border.

STEP 4: FRONT BORDER

With right side facing and holding border edge at top, transfer stitches from the two holders onto needle,

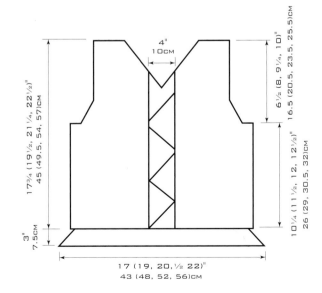

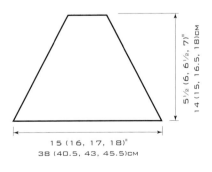

making sure to start with stitches on right side and end with those on left side. Attach yarn to right side, and work as follows:

Row 1: SKP, k to last st before center, k2tog (combining last stitch of right side with first stitch of left side), PM, k to end.

Row 2: SKP, k to marker, RM, k2tog, PM, k to end.

Repeat Row 2, inserting Long st row every 4th row, until 3 sts remain. Bind off all stitches. Cut yarn.

STEP 5: BACK BORDER

Work same as Step 4, to correspond to front border.

Tie

Thread a 34"/ 88cm length of yarn into tapestry needle. Starting at opening where center front border attaches to body, weave yarn in and out of each stitch opening all around border edge, ending back at center front. Remove needle and tie yarn ends into bow which can be tightened as needed.

This project was knitted with 5 (6, 7, 7) skeins of Artyarns 5-ply Cashmere, 100% cashmere medium weight yarn, 1.8oz/50g = 102yd/93m per skein, color #247, silver gray.

This variation was made using a simple lace pattern on the sleeves and neckline

Diagonals in Flight

![square bullet]

EXPERIENCE LEVEL
Intermediate

SIZES
X-Small (Small, Medium, Large)

THE FRONT BANDS OF THIS CARDIGAN ARE KNITTED ON THE DIAGONAL, AND FALL IN PLACE NICELY BECAUSE THE DIAGONAL GARTER STITCH GAUGE IS EQUIVALENT TO THAT OF THE STOCKINETTE LACE BODY STITCH. IT'S MEANT TO BE WORN LOOSELY OVER GARMENTS, SO THE PATTERN ALLOWS PLENTY OF EASE.

FINISHED MEASUREMENTS

Bust: About 36 (40, 44)"/92.5 (101.5, 111.5)cm

Total Length: 21½ (23, 25)"/54.5 (58.5, 63.5)cm

Loose fit (about 4"/10cm ease)

MATERIALS

Approx total: 1040 (1040, 1300)yd/952 (952, 1190)m silk and mohair/silk blend medium weight 2-strand yarn

Circular needles: 5mm (size 8 U.S.) *or size to obtain gauge*, at least 24"/61 cm long

Stitch marker

Stitch holder

Buttons with shanks, about ½"/1.3mm in diameter and small seed beads

Tapestry needle for finishing

Sewing needle and matching thread

GAUGE

16 sts and 20 rows = 4"/10cm in Lace Pattern

Always take time to check your gauge.

PATTERN STITCHES

Garter Stitch

Knit every row.

Left-leaning Lace Pattern

(multiple of 5 sts)

Note: When working odd-numbered rows, k across all extra stitches at the end of row when there are fewer than 5 sts and a full Lace Pattern repeat cannot be worked.

Row 1: ★Yo, SKP, k3; repeat from ★ across.

Row 2 and all even-numbered rows: Purl across.

Row 3: K1, ★yo, SKP, k3; repeat from ★ across, k any extra sts at end to last st (see note above), k1.

Row 5: K2, ★yo, SKP, k3; repeat from ★ across, k any extra sts to last st, k1.

Row 7: K3, ★yo, SKP, k3; repeat from ★ across, k any extra sts to last st, k1.

Row 9: K4, ★yo, SKP, k3; repeat from ★ across, k any extra sts to last st, k1.

Row 10: Purl across.

Repeat Rows 1 through 10 for pattern.

Right-leaning Lace Pattern

(multiple of 5 sts)

Note: When working odd-numbered rows, p across all extra stitches at the end of row when there are fewer than 5 sts and a full Lace Pattern repeat cannot be worked.

Row 1: *Yo, p2tog, p3; repeat from * across, p any extra sts at end to last st (see note above), k1.

Row 2 and all even-numbered rows: Knit across.

Row 3: P1, *yo, p2tog, p3; repeat from * across, p any extra sts to last st, k1.

Row 5: P2, *yo, p2tog, p3; repeat from * across, p any extra sts to last st, k1.

Row 7: P3, *yo, p2tog, p3; repeat from * across, p any extra sts to last st, k1.

Row 9: P4, *yo, p2tog, p3; repeat from * across, p any extra sts to last st, k1.

Row 10: Knit across.

Repeat Rows 1 through 10 for pattern.

Right/Left Lace Pattern

(multiple of 10 sts, plus 2 selvage sts)

Row 1: K1 (selvage), *k3, k2tog, yo; repeat from * to center marker, slip marker, **yo (working these meeting yo's, at center, by wrapping yarn twice around needle—once on each side of marker), SKP, k3; repeat from ** across to last st, k1 (selvage).

Row 2: K1, purl across, working inc 1 into double wrap of center yo (placing one st on each side of marker to maintain stitch count) to last st, k1.

Row 3: K3, k2tog, yo, *k3, k2tog, yo; repeat from * to last st before center marker, k1, slip marker, k1, **yo, SKP, k3; repeat from ** across, ending yo, SKP, k3.

Row 4: K1, purl across to last st, k1.

Row 5: K2, k2tog, yo, *k3, k2tog, yo; repeat from * to last 2 sts before marker, k2, slip marker, k2, **yo, SKP, k3; repeat from ** across, ending yo, SKP, k2.

Row 6: K1, purl across to last st, k1.

Row 7: K1, k2tog, yo, *k3, k2tog, yo; repeat from * to last 3 sts before marker, k3, slip marker, k3, **yo, SKP, k3; repeat from ** across, ending yo, SKP, k1.

Row 8: K1, purl across to last st, k1.

Row 9: K2tog, yo, *k3, k2tog, yo; repeat from * to 4 sts before marker, k4, slip marker, k4, **yo, SKP, k3; repeat from ** across, ending k2tog.

Row 10: K1, purl across to last st, k1.

Repeat Rows 1 through 10 for pattern.

INSTRUCTIONS

RIGHT FRONT

Cast on 36 (41, 46) sts. Cut yarn. Slide sts to other end of circular needle and attach yarn at other end of cast-on row, ready to work. Work back and forth in rows on circular needles.

Begin by working short rows as follows to establish diagonal front band:

Row 1: Inc 1, k1, turn; sl 1, k2.

Row 2: Inc 1, k3, turn; sl 1, k4.

Row 3: Inc 1, k5, turn; sl 1, k6—39 (44, 49) sts on needle.

Now work bottom border across all sts on needle as follows:

Row 4 (RS): Inc 1, k5, SSK, k across to end.

Row 5 (WS): K across to end.

Repeat Rows 4 and 5 once more.

Continue front band and begin Lace Pattern as follows:

Row 1 (RS): Inc 1, k6, SSK (front band sts), work Left-leaning Lace Pattern to end.

Row 2 (WS): K1, p to last 9 sts, k9.

Repeat these 2 rows until piece measures 13 (13½, 15)"/33 (34.5, 38)cm.

Armhole shaping

Starting at arm edge and maintaining continuity of pattern as established, bind off 4 sts once, then at same edge bind off 3 sts every other row once. Decrease 1 st at same edge every other row 3 times—29 (34, 39) sts.

Work even in pattern until piece measures 18 (18½, 20)"/45.5 (47, 50.5)cm, ending with a WS row.

V-neck shaping

Row 1: Starting at front neck edge, K8, SSK, work Lace Pattern (repeating directions for previous row) to end, turn; k1, p back to last 9 sts, k9 (note that front band has moved over by one stitch).

Rows 2 and 3: Repeat Row 1.

Row 4 (short row): K8, turn; sl 1, k7.

Repeat Rows 1–4 3 times more—17 (22, 27) sts.

Shoulder shaping

Work band sts and decrease as follows for shoulder shaping:

Row 1: SKP, k8, turn; sl 1, k to end.

Repeat Row 1 until 10 sts remain.

Next row: SKP, k6, SSK, turn; sl 1, k to end.

Following row: SKP, k4, SSK, turn; sl 1, k to end.

Next row: SKP, k2, SSK, turn; sl 1, k to end.

Following row: SKP, SSK, turn; SKP.

Cut yarn and fasten off.

LEFT FRONT

Cast on 36 (41, 46) sts. Work back and forth in rows on circular needles.

Begin by working short rows as follows to establish diagonal front band:

Row 1: Inc 1, k1, turn; sl 1, k2.

Row 2: Inc 1, k3, turn; sl 1, k4.

Row 3: Inc 1, k5, turn; sl 1, k6—39 (44, 49) sts on needle.

Row 4 (WS): Inc 1, k5, SSK, purl across to last st, k1.

Row 5: K1, p to last 9 sts, k9 (band sts).

Repeat Rows 4 and 5 once more.

Continue front band and begin Right-leaning Lace Pattern as follows:

Row 1 (WS): Inc 1, k6, SSK (front band), work Right-leaning Lace Pattern to last st, k1.

Row 2 (RS): K across.

Repeat these 2 rows until piece measures same length as Right Front to armhole.

Armhole shaping

Starting at arm edge and maintaining continuity of pattern as established, bind off 4 sts once, then at same edge bind off 3 sts every other row once. Decrease 1 st at same edge every other row 3 times—29 (34, 39) sts.

Work even in pattern until piece measures same as Right Front to V-neck, ending with a RS row.

V-neck shaping

Row 1: K8, SSK, work Lace Pattern (repeating directions for previous row) to end, turn; k back to end (front band has moved over by one stitch).

Rows 2 and 3: Repeat Row 1.

Row 4 (short row): K8, turn; sl 1, k7.

Repeat these 4 rows 3 times more—17 (22, 27) sts.

Shoulder shaping

Work same as for Right Front shoulder.

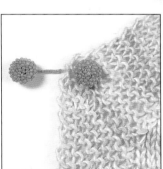

See page 89 for button closure instructions

BACK

Cast 72 (82, 92) sts onto circular needles. Work back and forth in rows on circular needles.

Knit 4 rows, placing a marker on needle at center of last row, 36 (41, 46) sts in from ends.

Work Right/Left Lace Pattern until piece measures same as fronts to armhole.

Armhole shaping

Keeping continuity of pattern as established, bind off 4 sts at beginning of next 2 rows, then bind off 3 sts at beginning of following 2 rows. Decrease 1 st at each end of every other row 3 times—52 (62, 72) sts.

Work even in Right/Left Lace Pattern, continuing to work a selvage st at each end, as before, until piece measures 20 (21½, 23½)"/51 (54.5, 59.5)cm.

Knit 8 rows. Bind off all sts for shoulders and back neck.

SLEEVES

Make 2.

Starting at wrist edge, cast on 36 (36, 42) sts.

Work back and forth on circular needles.

Knit 6 rows, placing a marker on needle at center of row, 18 (18, 21) sts in from ends.

Establish Right/Left Lace Pattern as follows:

Row 1: K1 (1, 4), k2tog, yo, *k3, k2tog, yo; repeat from * to center marker, slip marker, **yo (working these meeting yo's, at center, by wrapping yarn twice around needle—once on each side of marker), SKP, k3; repeat from ** across, ending yo, SKP, k1 (1, 4). First and last k sts are the selvage sts.

Row 2: K1, purl across, working inc 1 into double wrap of center yo (placing one st on each side of marker to maintain stitch count) to last st, k1.

Continue working pattern as established, with eyelets

shifting outward and a new eyelet pattern starting after every 10 rows as for the back, and at the same time, increase 1 st at each end of every 4th row 15 (0, 0), every 5th row 0 (12, 6), and every 6th row 0 (4, 9) times, working added sts in pattern. Then work even on 66 (68, 72) sts until sleeve measures 17 (18, 18½)"/43 (45.5, 47)cm.

Cap shaping

Keeping continuity of pattern, bind off 4 sts at beginning of next 2 rows, then bind off 3 sts at beginning of next 2 rows. Decrease 1 st at each end every other row 3 times—46 (48, 52) sts. Work even in pattern for 4 rows. Then decrease 1 st each end every row 6 times, then 1 st each end every other row 5 times—24 (26, 30) sts. Work even until cap measures 5¼ (6, 6¼)"/13.5 (15, 16)cm. Bind off 4 sts at beginning of next 2 rows, then bind off 2 sts at beginning of next 2 rows. Bind off remaining 12 (14, 18) sts.

FINISHING

Block all pieces to appropriate size. With right sides of fronts and back together, sew shoulder and side seams, aligning lace panels at seams. Sew underarm seam of each sleeve. Sew a sleeve to each armhole, matching

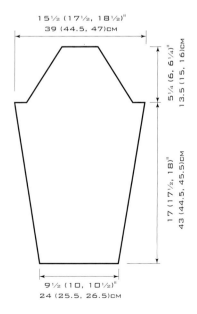

15½ (17½, 18½)"
39 (44.5, 47)cm

5¼ (6, 6¼)"/13.5 (15, 16)cm

17 (17½, 18)"/43 (44.5, 45.5)cm

9½ (10, 10½)"
24 (25.5, 26.5)cm

center top of cap to shoulder seam and matching sleeve seam to side seam at underarm.

Buttoned version (green cardigan)

On top of front band on Right Front, gently push stitches aside with a knitting needle tip to make a buttonhole. Repeat at corresponding position on Left Front. With sewing thread, stitch around opening to make a buttonhole. Link the two buttons together making several long stitches between them with sewing thread and stringing small seed beads so they are about 1"/2.5cm apart; to form a firm joining between the buttons. To close sweater at neckline, slip a button through each buttonhole.

This project was knit with 4 (4, 5) skeins of Art yarns Silk Rhapsody, 100% silk and 70% mohair/30% silk medium-weight 2-strand yarn, 3½oz/100g = 260yd/238m per skein, color #145, variegated pale blue (blue version) and color #2234, variegated pale green (green version).

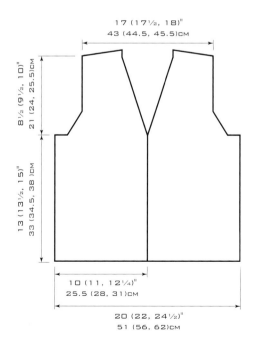

Modular Lace Part 2:

Simple
Center-Increase
Triangles

GET READY TO EXPERIENCE WHAT WONDERS SIMPLE CENTER-INCREASE TRIANGLES CAN DO FOR A GARMENT. IN THIS CHAPTER, YOU'LL LEARN HOW TO CREATE FIGURE-SLIMMING DESIGNS, EYE-CATCHING FLARED LACE TRIM, AND ATTRACTIVE KNITTED MATERIAL, ALL THROUGH THE MAGIC OF CENTER-INCREASE TRIANGLES.

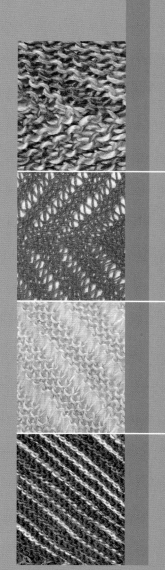

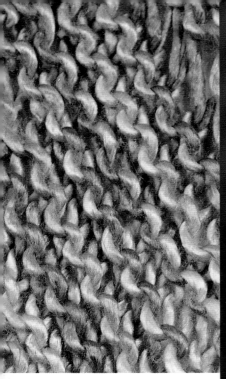

Three-In-One Aztec Sash

EXPERIENCE LEVEL

Easy

*J*ust one skein and a little bit of time can yield this must-have accessory. Imagine this sash with its tassels swinging jauntily from around the waist, artfully draped around a jacket collar, or woven into a modish up-do.

FINISHED MEASUREMENTS

About 4"/10cm wide x 48"/122cm long, plus 6"/15cm fringe at each end.

MATERIALS

Approx total: 163yd/149m silk lightweight yarn

Knitting needles: 2 pairs of 4mm (size 6 U.S.) *or size to maintain gauge*

Crochet hook: 3.25mm (size D/3 U.S.) for attaching fringe

Stitch marker

Stitch holders

GAUGE

16 sts and 32 rows = 4"/10cm in Garter Stitch

Always take time to check your gauge.

PATTERN STITCH

Garter Stitch

Knit every row.

Long Stitch

Knit each stitch wrapping yarn two times around needle to form 2 loops. On following row knit into first loop and drop second loop to form elongated stitch.

Long stitch is not worked in any increased or decreased stitches.

Long St Panel Pattern

Row 1: Inc 1, work Long st in each of next 11 sts, k2tog, work Long st into each of next 11 sts, p1.

Row 2: Knitting into only first wrap of double-wrapped sts and dropping second wrap, inc 1, k11, k2tog, k11, p1.

These 2 rows form a pattern panel.

INSTRUCTIONS

SASH

Note: Divide skein into two equal balls of yarn. You will be working each side separately from the center of the sash out to the end in 3 steps: center triangle, connecting triangles and extending straight side edges, and shaping the pointed end.

STEP 1: CENTER TRIANGLE

Make 2.

With one pair of needles, cast on 3 sts.

Row 1: Kl 1, inc 1, p1.

Row 2: Inc 1, inc 1, PM, k1, p1.

Row 3: Inc 1, k to marker, RM, inc 1, PM, k to last st, p1.

Repeat Row 3 until there are 26 sts on needle. Leaving working yarn attached, place stitches on a holder.

Make the second triangle in the same manner, and place stitches on another holder with yarn still attached.

STEP 2: CONNECTING TRIANGLES AND EXTENDING STRAIGHT SIDE EDGES

Starting with first triangle, transfer the 13 sts (half the stitches) closest to working yarn onto a needle. Then transfer 13 sts of second triangle farthest from working yarn onto the same needle, making sure to place center stitch on first, ending with edge stitch. Opposite 26 stitches should be transferred to holder.

Place working yarn and attached ball from one side into sealed bag, so it does not get in your way. You will be working just one side as follows:

Row 1: Inc 1, k11, k2tog, k11, p1.

Repeat Row 1 working Long St Panel every 6 rows until side edge measures 21"/53.5cm from center of Step 1 triangle. Leave stitches on needle.

With second set of needles, repeat Step 2 on remaining sts of center triangles to work other side of sash, until piece measures same length as first half.

STEP 3: SHAPING POINTED END

Continuing on sts at one end of sash, work as follows:

Row 1: K12, k2tog, PM, k to last st, p1.

Row 2: K to marker, RM, k2tog, PM, k to last st, p1.

Repeat Row 2 until 3 sts remain.

Last row: Sl 2, k1, pass each slipped stitch over the knitted stitch. Fasten off remaining stitch.

Repeat on other end of sash.

FINISHING

FRINGE
For each fringe, cut about 16 strands, each 12"/30.5cm long. Make a fringe at point of each end. (See page 18 for instructions on making fringe.)

This project was knit with 1 skein of Artyarns Regal Silk, 100% silk lightweight (DK) yarn, 1.8oz/50g =163yd/149m per skein, color #150, variegated golds and grays.

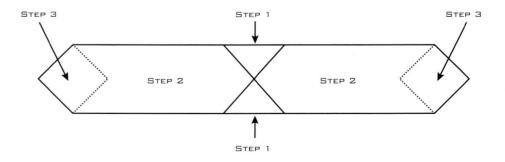

Chevron Ruana

EXPERIENCE LEVEL

Intermediate

SIZES

One size fits all.

SOFT FOLDS CASCADE DOWN THE FRONT OF THIS JACKET, WHILE THE BACK IS HOST TO A STRIKING DISPLAY OF KNIT ZIGZAGS. THE PATTERN IS ONE SIZE FITS ALL, AND THE DESIGN FLATTERS ALL FIGURES.

FINISHED MEASUREMENTS

Bust: About 69"/175.5cm at bust

Length at center back: About 30"/76cm

MATERIALS

Approx total: 1040yd/952m silk and mohair/silk blend medium-weight 2-strand yarn

Circular needles: 5mm (size 8 U.S.) *or size to obtain gauge*, 29 to 36"/73.5 to 91.5cm long

Crochet hook: 3.5mm (size E/4 U.S.)

5 stitch markers

2 stitch holders

GAUGE

12 sts and 24 rows = 4"/10cm in Garter Stitch

Always take time to check your gauge.

PATTERN STITCHES

Garter Stitch

Knit every row.

Long st

Row 1: Work edge stitches and increases and/or decreases as specified, but knit all knit stitches as long stitches by wrapping yarn around needle twice (instead of once) and drawing both loops through stitch. before for these sts).

Row 2: Work edge stitches and increases and/or decreases as specified, but knit only the first of the double wraps for each long st and drop the second to form the elongated st.

INSTRUCTIONS

Note: This project is knitted in 3 panels. Two panels are each worked for 2 steps: beginning center-increase triangle, then squared-off side section. A third panel is begun with a center-increase triangle in Step 3, then the 3 started panels are joined and worked in Step 4 to complete jacket.

PANEL 1

Cast on 3 sts. Work back and forth in rows on circular needle throughout.

STEP 1: BEGINNING TRIANGLE WITH CENTER INCREASES

Row 1: K1, inc 1, p1—4 sts.

Row 2: Inc 1, inc 1, k1, p1—6 sts.

Row 3: Inc 1, k 1, inc 1, PM, k2, p1—8 sts.

Row 4: Inc 1, k to marker, RM, inc 1, PM, k to last st, p1—2 sts increased.

Repeat Row 4 knitting Long St rows every 6 rows until base of triangle measures 12"/30.5cm across, ending with an even row (see Measuring Center-Increase Triangles on page 16).

STEP 2: SQUARED OFF TRIANGLE SIDES

Row 1: Continuing on triangle sts, k to marker, RM, inc1, PM, k to last 2 sts, p2tog

Repeat Row 1 knitting Long St rows every 6 rows until piece measures 16"/40.5cm from base of triangle, ending with an even row. Place all sts on to a stitch holder, maintaining marker in position. Cut yarn.

PANEL 2

Work same as for Panel 1, ending with stitches on holder and maintaining markers. Cut yarn.

PANEL 3

Cast on 3 sts.

STEP 3: BEGINNING TRIANGLE WITH CENTER INCREASES

Work narrower panel for center section as follows:

Repeat Step 1 for Panel 1 until base of triangle measures 10 ½"/26.5cm wide, ending with an even row. Slide Panel 3 stitches to center of circular needle. Cut yarn.

STEP 4: JOINING PANELS

Transfer stitches of Panel 1 onto end of needle, before Panel 3 sts, then transfer Panel 2 sts to other end of needle, keeping the Panel 3 sts in the middle; make sure all markers are in position. Attach yarn to edge of Panel 2 sts.

Work across all 3 panels on needle as follows:

Row 1: On Panel 2, k to marker, RM, inc 1, PM, k to last st of Panel 2, k2tog (combining 1 st each from Panels 2 and 3), PM; continuing on center Panel 3, k to marker, RM, inc 1, PM, k to last st of Panel 3, k2tog (combining 1 st each of Panels 3 and 1), PM; continuing on Panel 1, k to marker, RM, inc 1, PM, k to last 2 sts, p2tog.

Row 2: *K to marker, RM, inc 1, PM, k to marker, RM, k2tog, PM; repeat from * once, then k to marker, RM, inc 1, PM, k to last 2 sts, p2tog.

Repeat Row 2, inserting Long St rows every 6 rows to maintain pattern, until piece measures 47"/119.5cm from very beginning.

Bind off all sts. Cut yarn and weave in any loose yarn ends.

FINISHING

Fold Front section forward with right sides together. Seam side edges, using a backstitch, and leaving 11"/28cm open below shoulder fold for armholes. Turn right side out. Single crochet around all edges.

This project was knit with 4 skeins of Artyarns Silk Rhapsody, 100% silk and 70% mohair/30% silk blend, medium-weight 2-strand yarn, 3½oz/100g=260yd/238m per skein, color #2248, variegated browns.

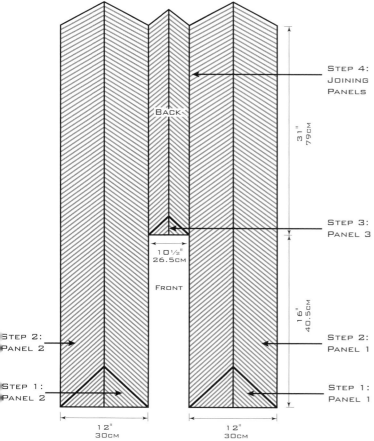

STEP 4:
JOINING
PANELS

BACK

31"
79CM

STEP 3:
PANEL 3

10½"
26.5CM

FRONT

16"
40.5CM

STEP 2:
PANEL 2

STEP 2:
PANEL 1

STEP 1:
PANEL 2

STEP 1:
PANEL 1

12"
30CM

12"
30CM

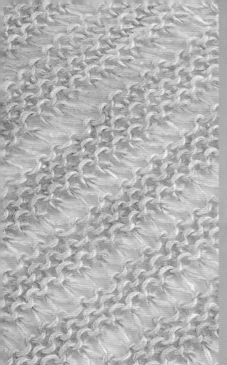

Long Stitch Wrap

■

EXPERIENCE LEVEL
Intermediate

SIZES
Small (Medium, Large)

SHRUGS HAVE BECOME A BASIC FASHION STAPLE, LENDING ELEGANCE TO ANY OUTFIT. THIS ONE HAS A DEEP NECKLINE AND FULL, FLOWING SLEEVES THAT DRAPE SOFTLY OVER BARE SHOULDERS, ALLOWING YOU TO MINGLE IN STYLE AT ANY SOCIAL GATHERING.

FINISHED GARMENT MEASUREMENTS

Note: Sizes are indicated here only to suggest how much yarn is needed, but the instructions allow you to customize the wraps to fit all sizes from small through large.

Bust: About 36 (40, 44)"/91.5 (101.5, 112)cm

Length: 14 (16, 18)"/35.5 (40.5, 45.5)cm

MATERIALS

Approx total: 520 (780, 1040)yd/476 (714, 952)m silk and mohair/silk blend medium-weight 2-strand yarn

Circular needles: 5mm (size 8 U.S.) *or size to obtain gauge, 24"/61cm long*

Stitch marker

Stitch holder

GAUGE

14 sts = 4"/10cm

PATTERN STITCH

Long Stitch

Knit each stitch wrapping yarn two times around needle to form 2 loops. On following row knit into first loop and drop second loop to form elongated stitch.

Long stitch is not worked in any increased or decreased stitches.

INSTRUCTIONS

Worked in 5 steps: Back triangle with center increases, first side panel, first triangular tie with center decreases, second side panel, second triangular tie. Throughout every 6 rows work a row of elongated sts, working the Long St into every k stitch in the row.

STEP 1: BACK TRIANGLE WITH CENTER INCREASES

Cast on 3 sts. Work back and forth in rows on circular needle throughout.

Row 1: Kl 1, inc 1, p1—4 sts.

Row 2: Inc 1, inc 1, PM, k1, p1—6 sts.

Row 3: Inc 1, k to marker, RM, inc 1, PM, k to last st, p1—2 sts increased.

Repeat Row 3 until triangle measures about 18 (20, 22)"/45.5 (50.5, 56)cm or desired width across base (see page 14 on how to measure the triangle base).

To measure triangle base accurately, remove stitches from needle as follows: Thread a tapestry needle with a length of yarn (at least 1 yd/.9m long). Draw threaded needle through the triangle sts and slide them off the needle. Lay triangle flat, but unstretched, and measure across base of triangle. Return the stitches to the needle, being careful to keep them in the proper order, with markers in position, and without twisting the stitches.

Now build height as follows:

Row 1: Sl 1, k to marker, RM, inc 1, PM, k to last st, p1.

Repeat Row 1 until piece measures about 14 (16, 18)"/35.5 (40.5, 45.5)cm, or desired height from top of neck to base.

STEP 2: FIRST SIDE PANEL

Now work each side separately as follows:

Remove marker and place the half of the stitches farthest from the working yarn on a holder. Work on remaining sts.

Row 1: Sl 1, k to last st, p1.

Repeat this row for about 14"/35.5cm or until wrap fits around shoulder, measured from the beginning of the panel at neck (point at top of triangle). End at neck edge.

STEP 3: FIRST TRIANGULAR TIE WITH CENTER DECREASES

Count the number of sts on your needle. Using Knitted Cast-on Method (see page 20), cast on an additional number of stitches equal to those already on the needle. Work across all sts as follows:

Row 1: K to last st of added group, k2tog (combining last added st with first previous st), PM, k to last 2 sts, p2tog.

Row 2: Sl 1, k to marker, RM, k2tog, PM, k to last 2 sts, p2tog.

Repeat Row 2 until only 4 sts remain.

Bind off all sts. Cut yarn and weave in ends.

STEP 4: SECOND SIDE PANEL

Transfer sts from holder and attach yarn to neck edge. Work to correspond to first side panel, following Step 2 directions.

STEP 5: SECOND TRIANGULAR TIE

Work to correspond to first triangular tie, following Step 3 directions.

FINISHING

On each side of garment, fold front tie forward along shoulder line, forming sleeve area at side edge. Be sure to get a comfortable fit for you, keeping the back area flat; then sew the underarm edges together for at least 3"/7.5cm to form the sleeves. The wider the side panels are, the longer the sleeve seam should be to fit well under the arms.

This project was knit with 2 (3, 4) skeins of Artyarns Silk Rhapsody, 100% silk and 70% mohair/30% silk blend medium-weight 2-strand yarn, 3½ oz/100g = 260yd/238m per skein, color #137, variegated beige.

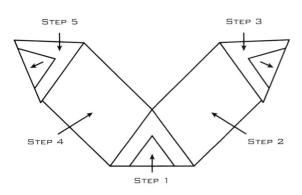

STEP 5   STEP 3

STEP 4   STEP 2

STEP 1

* SMALL ARROWS INDICATE DIRECTION OF KNITTING

Shapely Symmetry Sheath

EXPERIENCE LEVEL

Intermediate

SIZE

Small (Medium, Large, X-Large)

S AUNTER INTO A ROOM WEARING THIS
STUNNING DRESS, AND ALL EYES WILL BE
ON YOU. KNIT IN WHISPER-SOFT CASHMERE,
THE DARING NECKLINE, BOLD, ANGULAR
PATTERN, AND SELF-BELTED DESIGN ADD
TO THE HAUTE COUTURE LOOK.

FINISHED GARMENT MEASUREMENTS

Note: Measurements given below are for when this
form-fitting garment is actually worn, and includes
allowance for stretching. The garment, lying flat and
unstretched, will measure only about 28 (30, 32, 34)"/71
(76, 81, 86)cm at bust and hips.

Bust: 34 (38, 42, 46)"/86 (96, 107, 117)cm

Total length: 40 (41 1/2, 42 1/2, 44)"/104 (105.5, 108,
111.5)cm, unstretched

Hem to waist length: 23 (23 1/2, 23 1/2, 24)"/58.5
(59.5, 59.5, 61)cm, unstretched

Waist to shoulder length: 17 (18, 19, 20)"/43 (45.5, 48,
50.5)cm, unstretched

Snug Fit

MATERIALS

Approx total: 752 (940, 940, 940)yd/ 688 (860, 860,
860)m Merino wool medium-weight yarn (yarn A), and
510 (510, 765, 765)yd/467 (467, 700, 700)m cashmere
superfine yarn (yarn B) in variegated color, and
510 (510, 765, 765)yd/467 (467, 700, 700)m cashmere
superfine yarn (yarn C) in solid color

Circular needle: 5mm (size 8 U.S.) *or size to obtain gauge*, at
least 29"/73.5cm long

Crochet hook: 3.75mm (size F/5 U.S.)

Two 6mm glass beads for belt

Stitch markers

Stitch holders

Tapestry needle for finishing

GAUGE

17 sts and 34 rows = 4"/10cm in Garter Stitch, alternating
yarns A and B

Always take time to check your gauge.

PATTERN STITCHES

Garter Stitch

Knit every row.

INSTRUCTIONS

BACK

Note: The back is worked in 4 steps: two triangles that form the waist, section from waist to hem, squaring off the hem edge, and the neckline.

STEP 1: TRIANGLES AT WAIST

First triangle

With yarn A, cast on 3 sts. Work back and forth in rows on circular needle.

Row 1: With A, k1, inc 1, p1—4 sts.

Row 2: With A, inc 1, inc 1, PM, k1, p1—6 sts.

Row 3: With B, inc 1, k to marker, RM, inc 1, PM, k to last st, p1—8 sts.

Row 4: With B, inc 1, k to marker, RM, inc 1, PM, k to end. Drop B and pick up A.

Throughout, carry color not in use loosely along edge of work until it is needed again.

Repeat Rows 3 and 4, alternating yarns A and B every 2 rows until triangle measures 8½ (9½, 10½, 11½)"/21.5 (24, 26.5, 28)cm in height measured from cast-on sts to centermost st on needle, ending with a B ridge.

Transfer the stitches to a flexible stitch holder or waste yarn, removing original marker, and replacing it at the very midpoint of the sts on holder, with half the sts on one side of marker and half on the other side. Cut yarn.

Second triangle

Make another identical triangle, marking the center point as for the first triangle. Cut yarn B.

STEP 2: WAIST TO HEM SECTION

Following diagram, hold the two triangles with center markers facing each other. Place half the sts from one triangle (from point at base to center marker) onto needle, then place half the stitches from the second triangle (from center marker out to point at its base) on same needle, with working yarn A attached at tip of needle ready to knit. Keep remaining sts on triangles on their separate holders, removing the center markers.

Row 1: With A, inc 1, k to last st of first triangle, k2tog (combining last st of first triangle with first st of next triangle), PM, k to end.

Row 2: With A, inc 1, k to marker, RM, k2tog, PM, k to end.

Attach C. Repeat Row 2, alternating yarns A and C every 2 rows, until piece measures 14½ (15, 15, 15 ½)"/37 (38, 38, 39)cm from edge of first row (of Step 2) down side edge to skirt hem, ending with one A row.

STEP 3: SQUARING OFF HEM EDGE

Continue on same sts, working as follows:

Row 1: With A, k to marker, RM, k2tog, PM, k to last 2 sts, k2tog.

Attach C. Repeat Row 1, alternating A and C every 2 rows as before, until 3 sts remain. Bind off all 3 sts.

STEP 4: BACK NECKLINE SECTION

Transfer remaining triangle sts from holders onto circular needle, so that center sts (at point of each triangle) are next to each other at center of needle (see diagram). Attach A and with right side of work facing you, work as follows:

Row 1: With A, inc 1, k to center st of first triangle, k2tog (combining last st of first triangle with first st of next triangle), PM, k to end.

Row 2: With A, inc 1, k to marker, RM, k2tog, PM, k to end.

Attach C. Repeat Row 2, alternating A and C every 2 rows, until piece measures 17 (18, 19, 20)"/43 (45.5, 48, 50.5)cm from edge of waist to edge of shoulder, ending with a C ridge.

Shoulders and neck

Now square off piece for shoulders and work back neck edge as follows:

Row 1: With A, k to marker, RM, k2tog, k to last 2 sts, k2tog.

Repeat Row 1, alternating yarns as before, until there are 56 sts remaining.

Bind off all sts. Cut yarn.

FRONT

Repeat Steps 1 through 3 same as for Back.

STEP 4: FRONT NECKLINE SECTION

Work same as Step 4 for Back until piece measures 11½"/29cm from waist (see diagram), ending with a C ridge.

Cut A and attach B. Continue to work as before, repeating Row 2 of Step 4 for Back, but alternating B and C every 2 rows until piece measures 17 (18, 19, 20)"/43 (45.5, 48, 50.5)cm from edge of waist to edge of shoulder, ending with a C ridge.

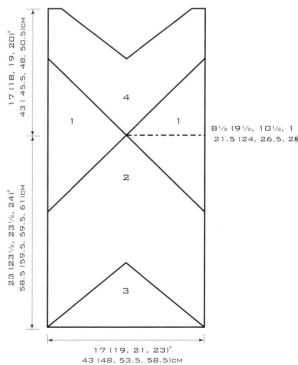

Shoulders and neck

Now square off piece for shoulders as follows:

Row 1: With B, k to marker, RM, k2tog, k to last 2 sts, k2tog.

Repeat Row 1, alternating B and C as before, until there are 66 sts remaining.

Bind off all sts loosely. Cut yarn.

FINISHING

With right sides of front and back together, sew shoulder seams, using yarn B and tapestry needle. Leaving a 7½ (8, 8½, 9)"/19 (20, 21.5, 23)cm opening below shoulder seam for armholes, and a 5"/12.5cm opening above hem edge for bottom slit, sew side seams. Cut yarn. Weave in yarn ends.

Drawstring cord for waist

Using about 5 yards of yarn A and crochet hook, crochet a chain as follows:

Leaving an 8"/20cm length of yarn unworked at beginning, ★chain 3, work single crochet (sc) into last chain made; repeat from ★ until crocheted section of cord measures about 46"/117cm. Fasten off and cut yarn, leaving an 8"/20cm end.

Thread one bead onto one end of cord, and knot end to hold bead in place. Weave other end in and out of eyelets at waist, starting at center front and working all around waistline to emerge again at center front. Thread other bead onto this end, and knot in place.

This project was knit with 4 (5, 5, 5)skeins of Artyarns Ultramerino 8, 100% Merino wool medium-weight yarn, 3 ½oz/100g = 188yd/172m per skein, color #233, deep green (yarn A), and2 (2, 3, 3) skeins of Artyarns Cashmere 2, 100% cashmere 2-ply superfine (fingering) yarn, 1.8oz/50g = 255yd/233m per skein, color #139, variegated green (yarn B), and 2 (2, 3, 3) skeins of Artyarns Cashmere 2, 100% cashmere 2-ply superfine (fingering) yarn, 1.8oz/50g = 255yd/233m per skein, color #233, deep green (yarn C).

BONUS PROJECT

WANT MORE USING THIS TECHNIQUE?
VISIT WWW.ARTYARNS.COM

Soiree Skirt

EXPERIENCE LEVEL

Intermediate

SIZE

Petite (Small, Medium, Large)

Use a simple stockinette stitch knit in a silk and mohair/silk blend to create the body of this clingy, leg-lengthening skirt, but the crowning glory of this piece is the lovely flared calf-length lace panel trim.

FINISHED GARMENT MEASUREMENTS

Note: Measurements given below are for when this form-fitting garment is actually worn, and includes about 12 inches of stretching. The garment, lying flat and unstretched, will measure only about 24 (26, 28, 30)"/61 (66, 71, 76)cm at hips.

Waist: About 28 (30, 32, 34)"/71 (76, 81, 86)cm

Hips: About 36 (38, 40, 42)"/91.5 (96.5, 101.5, 106.5)cm

Length: About 24 (24 1/2, 25, 25 1/2)"/61 (62, 63.5, 65)cm

Snug Fit

MATERIALS

Approx total: 780 (780, 1040, 1040)yd/714 (714, 952, 952)m silk and mohair/silk blend 2-strand medium-weight yarn (yarn A) and

163yd/149m silk lightweight yarn (yarn B) and 138yd/126m 1/8"/3mm-wide silk ribbon (yarn C)

Circular needles: 4.5mm (size 7 U.S.) *or size to obtain gauge*, 24"/61cm long

Knitting needle: 6.5mm (size 10 1/2 U.S.) for binding off

Small crochet hook

Stitch markers

4 stitch holders

1 yard of 1¼"/3cm-wide elastic for waistband

Sewing needle and sewing thread to match yarn

Tapestry needle for finishing

GAUGE

16 sts and 24 rows = 4"/10cm, unstretched, in Stockinette Stitch

Always take time to check your gauge.

PATTERN STITCHES

Stockinette Stitch in rows

Row 1 (RS): Knit across.

Row 2: Purl across.

Stockinette Stitch in rounds

Knit every round.

Openwork Pattern

(Even number of sts)

Row 1: ★Yo, SKP; repeat from ★ across.

Row 2: Knit across.

Repeat these 2 rows for pattern.

INSTRUCTIONS

SKIRT

Note: Skirt is worked in 3 steps: bottom triangles, joining triangles for bottom border, and skirt body.

STEP 1: BOTTOM TRIANGLES

Make 4 triangles, working as follows:

With yarn A, cast on 3 sts.

Row 1: With A, k1, inc 1, p1—4 sts.

Row 2: With A, inc 1, inc 1, PM, k1, p1—6 sts. Drop A and attach B.

Row 3: With B, inc 1, k to marker, RM, inc 1, PM, k to last stitch, p1—8 sts.

Row 4: With B, inc 1, k to marker, RM, inc 1, PM, k to last stitch, p1—10 sts. Drop B and pick up A. Continue to alternate yarns A and B, carrying color not in use loosely alongside edge of work.

Row 5: With A, inc 1, work Openwork Pattern to last st before marker, k1, RM, inc 1, PM, k1, work Openwork Pattern to last 2 sts, k1, p1.

Row 6: With A, inc 1, k to marker, RM, inc 1, PM, k to last st, p1.

Rows 7 through 34: Alternating yarns A and B every 2 rows, work as for Rows 5 and 6.

Rows 35 through 35 (37, 39, 41): Continuing to alternate yarns every 2 rows, inc 1, k to marker, RM, inc 1, PM, k to last st, p1—72 (76, 80, 84) sts.

Place sts on stitch holder, removing markers and cutting yarn. Repeat 3 more times for 4 triangles.

Leave last triangle made on one end of circular needle.

STEP 2: JOINING TRIANGLES

With last triangle still on one end of needle, transfer another triangle from holder to opposite end of circular needle, with right side of work facing you. Slide the triangles toward each other so the last st of first triangle is next to first st of following triangle.

★Attach yarn A to second triangle at its point where the two triangles meet. ★Working up the stitches of the second triangle to top point (at center) with A, k1, PM #1, k35 (37, 39, 41), turn. You will now be filling in the space between these 2 triangles, working short rows.

Row 1 (WS): Sl 1, PM #2, p to marker #1 (between triangles), RM, p2tog (combining last st of one triangle with first st of next triangle), PM #1, p35 (37, 39, 41) along edge of next triangle to top point (at center), turn.

Row 2 (RS): Sl 1, PM #3, k to last 2 sts before marker #1, SSK, RM, k1, PM #1, k2tog, k to marker #2, RM, turn.

Row 3: Sl 1, PM #2, p all sts to marker #3 (slipping marker #1 at center of row), RM #3, turn.

Repeat Rows 2 and 3 until only 3 active sts remain at center, removing markers #2 and #3. Cut yarn. Slip all the sts together with marker #1 in place to right-hand needle tip.

Transfer another triangle to the left-hand needle tip, sliding it toward the center to meet the previous triangle, and attach yarn to new triangle at its point where it meets the previous triangle's point. Repeat Step 2 to join new triangle to previously joined triangles. Then repeat once more to add last triangle to make the strip of 4 triangles.

Now to join the first and last triangles together to form a circle, being sure the stitches are not twisted around the needle and the pieces hang straight down. Repeat Step 2 to join the ends of the strip together.

STEP 3: SKIRT BODY

With yarn A, work in Stockinette Stitch in rounds, decreasing every 15th (16th, 17th, 18th) round 4 times as follows:

Decrease Round: ★K to 2 sts before marker, SSK, k1, k2tog; repeat from ★ 3 more times on round.

Work even until skirt measures 24 (24½, 25, 25½)"/ 61 (62, 63.5, 65)cm.

Bind-off Row: Using a larger-sized straight needle to work loosely, bind off all sts. Cut yarn.

Block skirt.

Duplicate crochet stitch

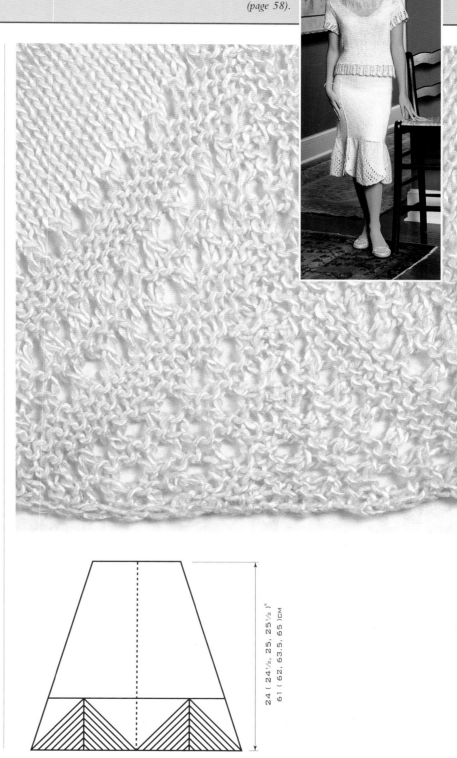

*Soiree Skirt paired with
Baby's Breath Tee
(page 58).*

Waistband

Cut length of elastic 2"/5cm longer than your waist measurement. Form circle, overlapping ends by 2"/5cm, and with sewing thread sew overlapping ends firmly together along edges. Place elastic circle just made inside skirt about 1½"/4cm below top of skirt. Fold under 1½"/4cm all around top of skirt, covering elastic to form casing for elastic, and pin skirt edge in place. Neatly sew edge of knitted fabric in place, being careful not to catch elastic in stitches.

Trim

Cut a 2-yard length of ribbon (yarn C) and thread it into tapestry needle. Starting at one side edge of front, weave ribbon in and out of elongated stitches formed around skirt body just above the triangle border; trim ribbon, leaving ends long enough to tie in a bow as shown.

With crochet hook and ribbon (yarn C), start at bottom of skirt to work a vertical line up the center stitch between decreases, working as follows: Hold ribbon against wrong side of skirt and, working from the right side, insert the crochet hook through the skirt to catch a loop of the ribbon on the hook and draw it through to the right side to form a chain stitch. Following the row of center stitches up to the top, work a row of chain stitches upward, drawing the loop for each new stitch through the previously made chain stitch, and covering the center stitches with the chain. Make a chain up each of the 4 vertical lines on the skirt. (See Decorative Duplicate Crochet Stitch, Page 19.)

Weave in yarn ends.

This project was knit with 3 (3, 4, 4) skeins of Artyarns Silk Rhapsody, 100% silk and 70% mohair/30% silk 2-strand medium-weight yarn, 3 1/2oz/100g = 260yd/238m per skein, color #221, pale yellow (yarn A), and 1 (1, 1, 1) skein of Artyarns Regal Silk, 100% silk lightweight yarn, 1.8oz/50g = 163yd/149m per skein, color #221, pale yellow (yarn B), and 1 (1, 1, 1) skein of Artyarns Silk Ribbon, 1/8"/3mm-wide 100% silk ribbon, .9oz/25g = 138yd/126m per skein, color #221, pale yellow (yarn C).

24 (24½, 25, 25½)"
61 (62, 63.5, 65)cm

Simple Center-Increase Triangles

Diagonal Lace Shell

![square]

EXPERIENCE LEVEL

Intermediate

SIZE

Small (Medium, Large, X-Large, XX-Large)

$\mathcal{F}$ THE FLATTERING SILHOUETTE OF THIS
TANK LOOKS GOOD ON ANY SHAPE AND
IS QUICK TO KNIT. WEAR IT ALONE, OR
SLIP IT UNDER A JACKET FOR DRAMATIC
OFFICE WEAR. MULTIDIRECTIONAL
KNITTING IS NEVER BORING, AND YOU'RE
SURE TO HAVE FUN WITH THIS ONE. KNIT
IT WITH OR WITHOUT SLEEVES.

FINISHED GARMENT MEASUREMENTS

Bust: About 35 (39, 43, 47, 51)"/89 (99, 109,119.5, 129.5)cm

Length to shoulder: 20 (22, 24, 26, 28)"/51 (56, 61, 66, 71)cm

MATERIALS

Approx total: 489 (652, 815, 978, 1141)yd/447 (597, 746, 894, 1044)m of silk lightweight yarn for sleeveless version as shown (to add optional sleeves, for which directions are given, purchase an additional 163yd/149m of same yarn).

Circular needles: 4mm (size 6 U.S.) *or size to obtain gauge,* 24"/61cm long

2 stitch holders

Stitch marker

Tapestry needle for finishing

GAUGE

20 sts and 44 rows (22 ridges) = 4" in Garter Stitch
Always take time to check your gauge.

PATTERN STITCHES

Garter Stitch

Knit every row.

UNUSUAL LACE FOR NECKLINE

3-St Dec—Worked over 3 sts. SSP, transfer remaining st back to left needle, pass second st on left needle over this new st (3 sts decreased to 1 st).

3-St Inc—Worked on 1 st remaining from decreases. ★K1 and leave original st on needle, transfer new st back to left needle, knit transferred st again (forming a new st on right needle); drop transferred st from left needle and keep original st on left needle. Working into original st again, repeat from ★ twice more (3 sts now on right needle); drop original st from left needle.

4-St Dec—Worked over 4 sts. SSP, ★sl 1, psso; transfer remaining st back to left needle, pass second st on left needle over this new st (4 sts decreased to 1 st).

4-St Inc—Worked in 1 st remaining from decreases. ★K1 and leave original st on left needle, transfer new st back to left needle, knit the transferred st again (forming a new st on right needle); drop transferred st from left needle and keep original st on left needle. Working into original st again, repeat from ★ 3 times more (4 sts now on right needle); drop original st from left needle.

5-St Dec—Worked over 5 sts. SSP, then sl 1, psso, transfer st back to left needle, pass second st on left needle over first st, then pass following st on left needle over first; (5 sts decreased to 1 st ready for increase).

5-St Inc—Worked in 1 st remaining from decreases. ★K1 and leave original st on left needle, transfer new st back to left needle, k the transferred new st again dropping the transferred st from the left needle (forming a new st on right needle); and keep the original st in place on the left needle. Working into the original st again, repeat from ★ 4 times more. There are now 5 sts on the right needle. Drop the original st from the left needle.

INSTRUCTIONS

FRONT

Note: The front is worked in 4 steps: lower front triangle with center increases, the right side section with short rows, the left side section worked to correspond, and the top neck section.

STEP 1: LOWER TRIANGLE

Cast on 3 sts.

Row 1: K1, inc 1, p1—4 sts.

Row 2: Inc 1, inc 1, PM, k1, p1—6 sts,

Row 3: Inc 1, k to marker, RM, inc 1, PM, k to last st, p1—2 sts increased.

Repeat Row 3 until base of triangle measures 17½ (19½, 21½, 23½, 25½)"/44.5 (49.5, 54.5, 59.5, 65)cm. If you are making the small size, make sure that you have a minimum of 120 sts on your needle.

Retain on the needle the side of the piece with the working yarn attached, and transfer the other half of the sts to a stitch holder, dividing the work between the center increase sts; remove the marker.

STEP 2: RIGHT SIDE

Continuing on the sts retained on needle, work short rows as follows:

Row 1: K to end, turn; inc 1, PM, k to last 2 sts, k2tog.

Note: From now on, you will be leaving an additional stitch unworked each time you turn (see page 13, Leaving Unworked Stitches in the center-increase triangle).

Rows 2 through 5: Sl 1, k to marker, RM, k1, turn; inc 1, PM, k to last 2 sts, p2tog.

Row 6: Sl 1, k2tog, k to marker, RM, k1, turn; inc 1, PM, k to last 2 sts, p2tog (extra decrease made for waist shaping).

Rows 7 through 21: Repeat Rows 2 through 6 three times more.

Rows 22 through 25: Sl 1, k to marker, RM, k1, turn; inc 1, PM, k to last 2 sts, p2tog.

Row 26: Sl 1, k to marker, RM, k1, turn; inc 1, PM, k to last st, p1 (extra increase made for waist shaping).

Rows 27 through 41: Repeat Rows 22 through 26 three times more.

Then repeat Rows 22 through 25, 0 (1, 2, 2, 2) times more.

Armhole shaping

Row 1: Sl 1, k2tog, k2tog, k to marker, RM, k1, turn; inc 1, PM, k to last 3 sts, k2tog, p1 (2 extra decreases for armhole).

Row 2: Repeat Row 1.

Rows 3 through 5: Sl 1, k2tog, k to marker, RM, k1, turn; inc 1, PM, k to last 3 sts, k2tog, p1 (extra decrease for armhole).

Row 6: Sl 1, k to marker, RM, k1, turn; inc 1, PM, k to last 3 sts, k2tog, p1.

Repeat Row 6 until there are 2 sts left before marker.

Next row: Sl 1, k1, RM, k1, turn; inc 1, p2tog.

Transfer all remaining sts onto a stitch holder, including 1 leftover st.

STEP 3: LEFT SIDE

Transfer the unworked sts of the other side of the lower triangle from the stitch holder to the needle. Attach yarn at upper point of triangle and inc1, PM, k to last 2 sts, k2tog.

Now work to correspond to step 2, starting with Row 2.

STEP 4: TOP NECK SECTION

Transfer sts from holders onto needle, placing a marker before and another after the center 5 stitches. Then counting from these markers, place another marker after each group of 5 sts as you count to outer edges. Allow 1 st at each outer edge of needle for the selvage st. With right side of work facing you, attach yarn to beginning of row.

Row 1: Slipping markers as you work row, inc 1, k to first marker, *work 5-St Dec (1 st remains on left needle), then work 5-St Inc into this remaining st; repeat from * to center 5 sts, work 5-St Dec, then 4-St Inc in remaining st; **work 5-St Dec, then 5-St Inc in the remaining st; repeat from ** to last marker, k to end.

Row 2: Continuing to slip markers, inc 1, p to last st, k1.

Row 3: Inc 1, k to first marker, *work 5-St Dec, then 5-St Inc in remaining st; repeat from * to center 4 sts, work 4-St Dec, then 3-St Inc in remaining st; **work 5-St Dec, then 5-St Inc in remaining st; repeat from ** to last marker, k to end.

Row 4: Repeat Row 2.

Row 5: Removing markers as you work across row, inc 1, k to first marker, *work 5-St Dec, then 5-St Inc in remaining st; repeat from * to center 3 sts, work 3-St Dec, then k1 leaving original st on left needle, transfer new st back to left needle, knit it again, dropping original st; **work 5-St Dec, then 5-St Inc in remaining st; repeat from ** to last marker, k to end.

Row 6: Repeat Row 2.

Divide work for shoulders

Row 1: K2tog, k16 (18, 20, 22, 24), turn; k2tog, k to end. Keeping these 16 (18, 20, 22, 24) sts on needle, place remaining sts on a stitch holder.

Continuing on these shoulder sts, work as follows:

Row 2: K2tog, k to end. Repeat this row until only 1 st remains. Fasten off.

Transfer sts from holder back onto needle. With right side of work facing you, attach yarn at beginning of row.

Bind off all sts until 17 (19, 21, 23, 25) sts remain; k these remaining sts.

Repeat Row 2 for previous shoulder until 1 st remains. Fasten off.

BACK

Work same as for Steps 1 through 3 for Front.

Transfer stitches from holders onto needle, placing a marker at centermost point of V.

With right side of work facing you, attach yarn at beginning of row.

Row 1: Inc 1, k to last st before marker, sl 1, RM, k1, psso, PM, k to end.

Rows 2 through 23: Repeat Row 1.

Shoulder and neck edge shaping

Row 24: K2tog, k to last st before marker, sl 1, RM, k1, psso, PM, k to end.

Repeat Row 24 until all stitches have been worked off. Fasten off.

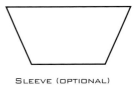

SLEEVE (OPTIONAL)

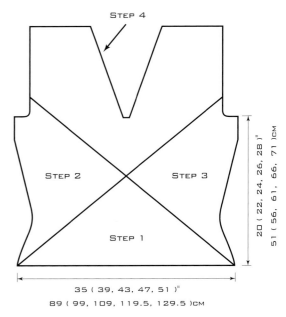

STEP 4

STEP 2   STEP 3

STEP 1

20 (22, 24, 26, 28)"
51 (56, 61, 66, 71)CM

35 (39, 43, 47, 51)"
89 (99, 109, 119.5, 129.5)CM

SHORT SLEEVES (OPTIONAL)

Make 2.

Note: Sleeves are worked beginning with the sleeve cap, which is formed from a triangle worked with center increases.

Cast on 3 sts.

Row 1: K1, inc 1, k1, turn—4 sts.

Row 2: Inc 1, inc 1, PM, k2—6 sts.

Row 3: Inc 1, k to marker, RM, inc 1, PM, k to end—2 sts increased.

Repeat Row 3 until you have 20 (20, 24, 24, 26) sts on needle.

Next row: K to marker, RM, inc 1, PM, k to end—1 st increased.

Repeat last row until you have 46 (50, 54, 58, 62) sts on needle.

Separate sides

Place half the sts furthest from the working yarn on a stitch holder.

First side

Work on remaining 23 (25, 27, 29, 31) sts as follows:

Row 1: K to last st, sl 1, turn; SSP, k to end.

Repeat Row 1 until 14 (16, 18, 20, 22) sts remain.

Now square off sides as follows:

Row 1: K to last st, sl 1, turn; SSP, k to last 2 sts, k2tog.

Repeat Row 1 until 2 sts remain. Bind off.

Second side

Attach yarn at top of triangle.

Next row: SSP, k to end.

Now complete to correspond to first side, repeating Row 1, then squaring off sides.

FINISHING

With right sides together, sew shoulder and side seams. Work a row of single crochet (sc) around V-neck, bottom edge, and, for sleeveless version, around armholes, spacing stitches to keep edges smooth and flat. Weave in yarn ends.

For sleeves

Block sleeves. Sew underarm seams (squared-off sides) of sleeves. Turn garment inside out. With right sides together, pin a sleeve to each armhole, matching center top of sleeve cap to shoulder seam and sleeve seam to underarm seam of garment; ease the cap to fit around the armhole smoothly. Sew sleeve to armhole, using backstitch. Weave in yarn ends.

This project was knit with 3 (4, 5, 6, 7) skeins for sleeveless version, or 4 (5, 6, 7, 8) skeins for sleeved version, of Artyarns Regal Silk, 100% silk lightweight yarn, 1.8oz/50g = 163yd/149m per skein, color #218, rust red.

Silky Tie Wrap

EXPERIENCE LEVEL

Intermediate

SIZE

Small (Medium, Large)

WHETHER KNOTTED OR LEFT OPEN, THIS IS A PERFECT COVER-UP FOR A SLEEVELESS TANK TOP OR DRESS. THE WRAP IS CONSTRUCTED IN SUCH A WAY THAT YOU CAN MAKE IT TO FIT EXACTLY. YOU MAY FIND THIS TYPE OF KNITTING ADDICTIVE.

FINISHED MEASUREMENTS

This wrap is knitted proportionally. The width of the first (center) triangle determines the size of the entire wrap. Carefully measure across the back from underarm to underarm, allowing 2"/5cm extra for ease on each side, and make the base of the first triangle wide enough to cover the entire back.

Width range from Small (approx 23"/58.5cm) to Large (approx 30"/76cm) across back.

Length range from Small (9"/23cm) to Large (12"/30.5cm)

MATERIALS

Note: Use middle number for mid-range size.

Approx total: 489 (652, 815)yd/447 (597, 746)m silk lightweight yarn

Circular needles: 4.5mm (size 7 U.S.) *or size to obtain gauge*, at least 24"/61cm long

Stitch marker

Stitch holder

Tapestry needle for finishing

GAUGE

18 sts and 28 rows = 4"/10cm in Pattern Stitch

Always take time to check your gauge.

Simple Center-Increase Triangles

INSTRUCTIONS

WRAP

Note: This wrap is worked in three steps: back center-increase triangle, side panel, and triangular tie section to complete one side, then steps 2 and 3 are repeated on other side of Step 1 triangle. Every 6 rows work a row where every k stitch is a Long St. On the subsequent row work only into the first wrap of the Long St (see page 10).

STEP 1: BACK TRIANGLE

Work as for Long Stitch Wrap, page 100.

STEP 2: FIRST SIDE PANEL

Work as for Long Stitch Wrap, page 100.

STEP 3: TRIANGULAR TIE SECTION

Continuing on bottom edge of side panel sts (same edge as cast-on edge), work as follows:

Row 1: Inc 1, SKP, turn; sl 1, k to last st, p1.

Row 2: Inc 1, k1, SKP, turn; sl 1, PM, k to last st, p1.

Row 3: Inc 1, k to marker, RM, SKP, turn; sl 1, PM, k to last st, p1.

Rows 4 through 5: Repeat Row 3.

Row 6: Inc 1, work Long sts to marker, RM, SKP, turn; knitting only first wrap of Long sts as before, sl 1, PM, k to last st, p1.

Repeat Rows 3 through 6 until triangle has used up all sts from the side panel.

Bind off loosely. Cut yarn.

SECOND SIDE

Transfer stitches from stitch holder onto needle and attach yarn to top of other side (neck edge of Step 1 [back] triangle).

Repeat Steps 2 and 3 to complete second side.

FINISHING

Cut yarn and weave in yarn ends.

Fold one side panel in half lengthwise so its outer-edge corners meet. Thread tapestry needle with yarn and sew these two corners together with two or three neat stitches to form arm opening. Repeat on other side.

To wear this wrap, slip the stitched corners underneath your arms and tie the two triangles together across the front. The first step triangle should lie flat across the back.

This project was knitted with 3 (4, 5) skeins of Artyarns Regal Silk, 100% silk, lightweight yarn, 1.8oz/50g = 163yd/149m per skein, color #251, red.

STEP 3   STEP 3

STEP 2   STEP 2

STEP 1

FOLD TO BRING
TWO CORNERS
TOGETHER

FOLD TO BRING
TWO CORNERS
TOGETHER

WIDTH EQUALS ARMHOLE TO
ARMHOLE MEASUREMENT
ACROSS BACK, PLUS 2"/5CM EASE

MODULAR LACE
PART 3:

LACY
CENTER-
INCREASE
TRIANGLES

$\mathscr{Y}$OUR FRIENDS AND FAMILY WILL UNDOUBTEDLY BE QUITE IMPRESSED WHEN YOU INCORPORATE A LACE REPEAT INTO A MODULAR PATTERN. BUT HAVE NO FEAR, THE STITCHES ONLY LOOK COMPLICATED. THEY'RE A BREEZE TO EXECUTE ONCE YOU GET THE HANG OF THEM.

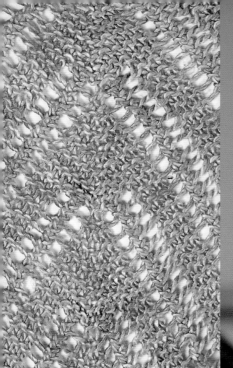

Filigree Wrap

*Silk version using
one yarn.*

WHEN KNIT IN SILK ALONE, THIS EXQUISITE WRAP LOOKS COMPLETELY DIFFERENT FROM WHEN THE SILK IS ALTERNATED WITH MOHAIR, BUT EITHER WAY THE RESULTS ARE REMARKABLE. CAN'T DECIDE? MAKE ONE OF EACH!

MATERIALS

Approx total: 163yd/149m silk lightweight yarn (yarn A), and

Approx total: 230yd/210m mohair and silk blend superfine (yarn B), *or*

Approx total: 489yd/447m silk lightweight yarn only (yarn A) for all silk version

Knitting needles: 4.5mm (size 7 U.S.) *or size to obtain gauge*

Stitch marker

GAUGE

14 sts and 32 rows = 4"/10cm in Lace Pattern

Always take time to check your gauge.

PATTERN STITCH

LP: yo, sl1, k2tog, psso, yo

Lace Pattern

for checking gauge only

(Multiple of 6 sts, plus 3)

Row 1: K3, ★LP, k3; repeat from ★ across.

Row 2: K across.

Repeat these 2 rows for lace pattern.

Silk alternated with mohair two yarn version.

INSTRUCTIONS

SHAWL

Note: This shawl is worked in 3 steps: forming the beginning triangle, working the center section with straight edges, and squaring off the end section.

STEP 1: BEGINNING TRIANGLE WITH CENTER INCREASES

Starting with yarn A, cast on 3 sts.

Row 1 (RS): With A, k1, inc 1, p1—4 sts.

Row 2: Inc 1, inc 1, k1, p1—6 sts. Drop A and attach B.

Note: For all-silk version, continue with A only thoughout; for 2-yarn version from now on, alternate yarns A and B every 2 rows, carrying the yarn not in use loosely up the side of your work.

Row 3: With B, inc 1, k1, inc 1, k2, p1—8 sts.

Row 4: With B, inc 1, k2, inc 1, k3, p1—10 sts.

Row 5: With A, inc 1, LP, inc 1, LP, k1, p1—12 sts.

Row 6: With A, inc 1, k4, inc 1, k5, p1—14 sts.

Row 7: With B, inc 1, k1, LP, k1, inc 1, k1, LP, k2, p1—16 sts.

Note: Frequently check your knitting to make sure each LP lines up over the one from the previous pattern row. Each LP forms in the previous row's grouping of 3 lace sts—easily seen from the eyelet holes.

Notice also that LP are worked on odd-numbered (right-side) rows and sts are knitted on even-numbered (wrong-side) rows throughout. See Traveling Lace on page 8.

Row 8: With B, inc 1, k6, inc 1, k7, p1—18 sts.

Row 9: With A, inc 1, k2, LP, k2, inc 1, k2, LP, k3, p1—20 sts.

Row 10: With A, inc 1, k8, inc 1, k9, p1—22 sts.

Row 11: With B, inc 1, k3, LP, k3, inc 1, k3, LP, k4, p1—24 sts.

Row 12: With B, inc 1, k10, inc 1, k11, p1—26 sts.

Row 13: With A, inc 1, k4, LP, k4, inc 1, k4, LP, k5, p1—28 sts.

Row 14: With A, inc 1, k12, inc 1, k 13, p1—30 sts.

Row 15: With B, inc 1, k5, LP, k5, inc 1, k5, LP, k6, p1—32 sts.

Row 16: With B, inc 1, k14, inc 1, k15, p1—34 sts.

Note: New LP (lace panels) are added whenever there are 6 k sts on either side of previous LP (not counting edge inc or p sts or center inc or ktog sts), as on next row. The LP must always have 3 knit sts between it and another LP. However, 3 k sts are not required between a lace panel and the edge or center sts.

Row 17: With A, inc 1, work (LP, k3) twice, LP, inc 1, work (LP, k3) twice, LP, k1, p1—36 sts.

Row 18: With A, inc 1, k16, inc 1, PM, k17, p1—38 sts.

Row 19: With B, inc 1, work LP pattern as set to marker, RM, inc 1, PM, work LP pattern as set to last st, p1.

Row 20: With B, inc 1, k to marker, RM, inc 1, PM, k to last st, p1.

Repeat Rows 19 and 20, alternating A and B every 2 rows as before, and remember to insert new Lace Panels as needed whenever there are 6 knit sts between the last LP and the edge sts or center sts; work until shawl measures about 12"/30.5cm wide, unstretched.

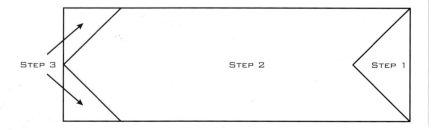

STEP 2: STRAIGHT CENTER SECTION

Note: As the 3-stitch Lace Panels reach the straight edges of the scarf, discontinue the LP and knit across the remaining sts. New Lace Panels will continue to be formed at the center of the rows as the old ones are worked off at the edges.

Continue to alternate yarns as before and square off side of shawl as follows:

Row 1: K1, work Lace Panels as set to marker, RM, inc 1, PM, work Lace Panels as set to last 2 sts, p2tog.

Row 2: K to marker, RM, inc 1, PM, k to last 2 sts, p2tog.

Repeat these 2 rows and continue to insert new Lace Panels as needed (see note following Row 16 in Step 1), until shawl measures 40"/101.5cm long, unstretched, or desired length (allowing enough yarn to complete Step 3).

STEP 3: SQUARING OFF END SECTION

Continue to alternate yarns as before and square off top, working each corner separately as follows:

Row 1: K1, work Lace Panels as set to marker, RM, k1, turn, SKP, PM, k to last 2 sts, p2tog.

Repeat this row, decreasing sts each row until 2 sts remain.

Bind off last 2 sts. Cut yarn.

For second corner, attach yarn to other side at top edge. K to last 2 sts, p2tog, then repeat Row 1 as for first corner until only 2 sts remain.

Bind off last 2 sts. Cut yarn. Weave in yarn ends.

This project was knitted with 1 skein of Artyarns Regal Silk, 100% silk, lightweight yarn, 1.8oz/50g = 163yd/149m per skein, color #215, pink (yarn A), and 1 skein Artyarns Silk Mohair, 70% mohair/30% silk, superfine weight yarn, .9oz/25g = 230yd/210m per skein, color #130, variegated pink and brown (yarn B).

Alternate version was knit with 3 skeins of Artyarns Regal Silk, 100% silk, lightweight yarn, 1.8oz/50g = 163yd/149m per skein, color #105, pinks and greens.

Perfect Choice Sweater

■

WHETHER IT'S A GALLERY OPENING, LUNCH DATE, OR AN EVENING AT THE MOVIES, THIS FIGURE-FLATTERING SWEATER IS THE PERFECT TOP TO WEAR. IT'S A UNIQUE PIECE THAT IS KNITTED ENTIRELY ON ANGLES, WITH LACE PANELS PERPENDICULAR TO THE KNITTED ONES.

FINISHED MEASUREMENTS

Bust: 34 (37, 40, 43, 46, 49)"/86 (94, 101.5, 109)(117, 124.5)cm

Total length: 21 (21½, 22, 23½)(24, 25)"/53.5 (54.5, 56, 59.5)(61, 63.5)cm

Standard fit

MATERIALS

Approx total: 1040 (1040, 1300, 1300)(1560, 1560)yd/952 (952, 1190, 1190)(1428, 1428)m

silk and mohair/silk blend medium-weight 2-strand yarn

Circular needle: 5mm (size 8 U.S.) *or size to obtain gauge*, at least 24"/61cm long.

Crochet hook: 3.5mm (size E/4 U.S.)

Set of stitch marker, including some clip-on markers (similar to safety pins, shown on page 15)

Stitch holders

Tapestry needle for finishing

GAUGE

14 sts and 20 rows = 4"/10cm in Lace Pattern

Always take time to check your gauge.

PATTERN STITCH

Pattern Notes: As in the Filigree Wrap (page 126), Lace Panels are established in the first 16 rows. Continue to work Lace Panels as set, checking your knitting to make sure each LP lines up over the one from the previous pattern row. Add new Lace Panels as needed whenever ther are 6 knit sts between the last LP and the edge or center sts. When decreasing in pattern, discontinue working a Lace Panel when there are not enough sts to work the full 3-stitch pattern, and knit these sts instead. There should always be 3 knit sts between Lace Panels.

LP: yo, sl1, k2tog, psso, yo

Lace Pattern *for checking gauge only*

Row 1 (RS): K3, ★LP, k3; repeat from ★ across.

Row 2: Knit across.

Repeat Rows 1 and 2 for pattern.

SHAPING PATTERNS GLOSSARY

Back Even Ridge Pat:

Row 1: K1, work Lace Pat as established to marker, RM, inc 1, PM, work Lace Pat as established to last 2 sts, k2tog

Row 2: K to marker, RM, inc 1, PM, k to last 2 sts, k2tog

Back Decrease Ridge Pat:

Row 1: K2tog, work Lace Pat as established to marker, RM, inc 1, PM, work Lace Pat as established to last 2 sts, k2tog

Row 2: K2tog to marker, RM, inc 1, PM, k to last 2 sts, k2tog

Back Increase Ridge Pat:

Row 1: K1, work Lace Pat as established to marker, RM, inc 1, PM, work Lace Pat as established to last st, k1

Row 2: K to marker, RM, inc 1, PM, k to last st, k1

Left Side Even Ridge Pat:

K1, work Lace Pat as established to marker, RM, k1, turn; inc 1, PM, k to last 2 sts, k2tog

Left Side Decrease Ridge Pat:

K2tog, work Lace Pat as established to marker, RM, k1, turn; inc 1, PM, k to last 2 sts, k2tog

Left Side Increase Ridge Pat:

K1, work Lace Pat as established to marker, RM k1, turn; inc 1, PM, k to last st, k1

Right Side Even Ridge Pat:

Inc 1, PM, work Lace Pat as established to last 2 sts, k2tog, turn; k to marker, RM, k1, turn

Right Side Decrease Ridge Pat:

Inc 1, PM, work Lace Pat as established to last 2 sts, k2tog, turn; k2tog, k to marker, RM, k1, turn

Right Side Increase Ridge Pat:

Inc 1, PM, work Lace Pat as established to last st, k1, turn; k to marker, RM, k1, turn

INSTRUCTIONS

BACK

Back is in worked 4 steps: Beginning triangle with center increases to establish width, shaping side edges, armhole shaping, and separating for shoulders.

STEP 1: BACK WIDTH

Cast on 3 sts

Work Rows 1 to 20 of Filigree Wrap on page 126 with single yarn (ignore all reference to A and B). Continue to alternate Rows 19 to 20 until there are 70 (80, 90, 100) (110, 118) sts.

STEP 2: WAIST SHAPING

Then work 2 (2, 3, 3) (3, 4) Back Even Ridge Pat (see Shaping Patterns Glossary), repeating rows 1-2 for each ridge. Decrease for waist with [1 Back Decrease Ridge Pat, followed by 2 Back Even Ridge Pat] worked 3 times—64 (74, 84, 94) (104,112) sts.

Then work 8 (8, 8, 9) (9, 10) Back Even Ridge Pat, repeating rows 1-2 for each ridge.

Increase for waist with [1 Back Increase Ridge Pat, and 2 Back Even Ridge Pat] worked 3 times— 70 (80, 90, 100) (110, 118) sts.

Now work Back Even Ridge Pat for 2 (2, 2, 3) (4, 4) times or until work measures 12 (12, 12½, 13½) (13½, 14)"/30.5 (30.5, 32, 24) (34, 35.5)cm from bottom edge.

STEP 3: ARMHOLE SHAPING

Row 1: Bind off 2 sts, work Lace Pat as set to marker, RM, inc 1, PM, work Lace Pat as set to last 2 sts, k2tog.

Row 2: Bind off 2 sts, k to marker, RM, inc 1, PM, k to last 2 sts, k2tog.

Repeat these last 2 rows 2 (2, 3, 3) (4, 5) times more. Work Even ridge for 5 (5, 2, 0), (0, 0) times.

STEP 4: SEPARATE FOR SHOULDERS

Right Shoulder

Row 1 (RS): Starting at right shoulder, bind off 0 (0, 0, 0) (2, 3) sts, k1, work Lace Pat to marker, RM, k1.

Place remaining sts on a stitch holder. Turn to work back across right shoulder sts.

Row 2: SKP, k to last 2 sts, k2tog

Row 3: Bind off 0 (0, 0, 0) (0, 3) sts, k1, work Lace Pat to last st, k1

Row 4: SKP, k to last 2 sts, k2tog

Row 5: K1, work Lace Pat to last st, k1

Row 6: SKP, k to last 2 sts, k2tog

Repeat Rows 5 and 6 until 2 or 3 sts remain. Bind off all sts. Cut yarn.

Left Shoulder

Transfer sts from holder to needle. Attach yarn at neck edge.

Row 1 (RS): SKP, work Lace Pat as set to last 2 sts, k2tog.

Row 2: Bind off 0 (0, 0, 0) (2, 3) sts, k to marker, RM, k1, turn.

Row 3: SKP, work Lace Pat to last 2 sts, k2tog.

Row 4: Bind off 0 (0, 0, 0) (0, 3) sts, k to end.

Row 5: SKP, work Lace Pat as set to last 2 sts, k2tog.

Row 6: K across.

Repeat Rows 5 and 6 until 2 or 3 sts remain. Bind off all sts. Cut yarn.

FRONT

Front is worked in 7 steps: Bottom triangle for width, beginning waist shaping, separating left and right sides, continuing left side shaping, neckline and armhole, continuing right side shaping, neckline and armhole, V-neckline.

STEP 1: FRONT WIDTH

Repeat Step 1 of Back until there are 70 (80, 90, 100) (110, 118) sts.

STEP 2: BEGINNING OF WAIST SHAPING

Then work 2 (2, 3, 3) (3, 4) Back Even Ridge Pat, repeating rows 1-2 for each ridge. Decrease for waist

with [1 Back Decrease Ridge Pat, and 2 Back Even Ridge Pat] worked 1 time—68 (78, 88, 98) (108, 116) sts.

STEP 3: SEPARATE LEFT AND RIGHT SIDES

With right side facing, place half the stitches farthest away from the working yarn on a stitch holder—34 (39, 44, 49) (54, 58) sts remain. You will now be leaving stitches behind to form V neckline as shown on page 15.

STEP 4: LEFT SIDE

Continue Decrease for Waist Shaping

K2tog, work Lace Pat as set to last st, k1, turn; inc1, PM, k to last 2 sts, k2tog.

Now work Left Side Even Ridge Pat 2 times. Then work Left Side Decrease Ridge Pat one time, followed by 10 (10, 10, 11) (11, 12) Left Side Even Ridge Pat.

Increase for Waist Shaping

Work [Left Side Increase Ridge Pat followed by 2 Left Side Even Ridge Pat] 3 times. Now work Left Side Even Ridge Pat 2 (2, 2, 3) (4, 4) more times.

Left Armhole Shaping

Row 1: Bind off 2 sts, work Lace Pat as set to marker, RM,1, turn; inc 1, PM, k to last 2 sts, k2tog.

Repeat Row 1 for 2 (2, 3, 3) (4, 5) times more.

> For sizes X-Large and XX-Large only:
>
> **Row 1:** Bind off 0 (0, 0, 0) (2, 3), k1, work Lace Pat to marker, RM, k1, turn; inc 1, PM, k to last 2 sts, k2tog.
>
> **Row 2:** Bind off 0 (0, 0, 0) (0, 3), k1, work Lace Pat to marker #w, RM, k1, turn; inc 1, PM, k to last 2 sts, k2tog

> For all sizes:

Work Left Side Even Ridge until 1 or 2 sts remain to the left of marker. K across these sts to armhole edge. Cut yarn. Place left side stitches on stitch holder.

STEP 5: RIGHT SIDE

Transfer right side stitches to needle, attaching yarn to stitch at center of work (furthest away from edge)

Continue Decrease for Waist Shaping

Work [Right Side Decrease Ridge Pat followed by 2 Right Side Even Ridge Pat] 2 times.

Then work an additional 8 (8, 8, 9) (9, 10) Right Side Even Ridge Pat.

Increase for Waist Shaping

Work [Right Side Increase Ridge Pat followed by 2 Right Side Even Ridge Pat] 3 times. Then work an additional 2 (2, 2, 3) (4, 4) Right Side Even Ridge Pat.

Right Armhole Shaping

Row 1: Inc 1, PM, work Lace Pat as set to last 2 sts, k2tog, turn; bind off 2 sts, k to marker, RM, k1, turn

Repeat Row 1 for 2 (2, 3, 3) (4, 5) times more.

For sizes X-Large and XX-Large only:

Row 1: Inc 1, PM, work Lace Pat as set to last 2 sts, k2tog, turn; bind off 0 (0, 0, 0) (2, 3) sts, k to marker, RM, k1, turn

Row 2: Inc 1, PM, work Lace Pat as set to last 2 sts, k2tog, turn; bind off 0 (0, 0, 0) (0, 3) sts, k to marker, RM, k1, turn

For all sizes:

Work Right Side Even Ridge Pat until 1 or 2 sts remain to the right of marker. K across these sts to armhole edge, ending with all sts on right-hand side of needle.

STEP 6: V NECKLINE

Transfer Left Side stitches from stitch holder onto needle. At this point, use clip-on stitch markers to plan the lace panels from the center out so that they are completely centered. Allowing 2 center most stitches (1 from left side and 1 from right side), space stitch markers 3 stitches out from 2 center stitches in either direction. Symmetry is important here, so it is essential that the lace ridges be planned in advance.

Begin knitting at armhole edge of right front where working yarn is attached.

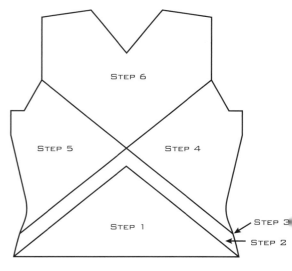

FRONT

Row 1: Inc 1, work Lace Pat as established by markers to last st of right front, k2tog (combining last st of right front and first st of left front), place marker, work Lace Pat as established by markers to last st, k1—you can now remove all clip-on stitch markers as lace has been established, leaving only the center marker to identify decrease at center.

Row 2: Inc 1, k to marker, RM, k2tog, PM, k to end.

Row 3: Inc 1, work Lace Pat as established to marker, RM, k2tog, PM, work Lace Pat as established to last st, k1.

Row 4: Inc 1, k to marker, RM, k2tog, PM, k to end.

Repeat Rows 3-4 until armholes measure same length as for back armholes.

Shoulder Shaping

Row 1: K1, work Lace Pat as set to marker, RM, k2tog, PM, work Lace Pat as set to last st, k1

Row 2: K to marker, RM, k2tog, PM, k to end

Repeat these rows a total of 8 (9, 10, 11) (12, 13) times. Bind off all sts.

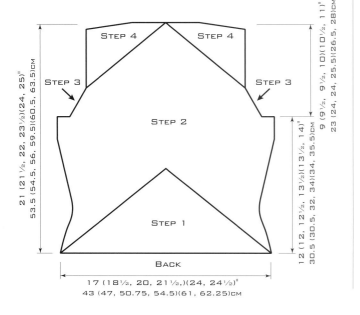

21 (21½, 22, 23½)(24, 25)"
53.5 (54.5, 56, 59.5)(60.5, 63.5)CM

STEP 4   STEP 4

STEP 3   STEP 3

STEP 2

STEP 1

BACK

17 (18½, 20, 21½,)(24, 24½)"
43 (47, 50.75, 54.5)(61, 62.25)CM

12 (12, 12½, 13½)(13½, 14)"
30.5 (30.5, 32, 34)(34, 35.5)CM

9 (9½, 9½, 10)(10½, 11)"
23 (24, 24, 25.5)(26.5, 28)CM

SLEEVES

Make 2.

Note: Sleeves begin at cap and are worked down to wrist.

Cast on 3 sts.

Rows 1 through 8: Work same as for first 8 rows of Step 1 on Back, placing a marker on needle after center increase as you work the last row (18 sts for all sizes).

Now the following ridges will be used to shape the sleeve; directions for using the ridges follow these explanations:

Single Increase Ridge

Row 1: K1, work Lace Pattern as set to marker, RM, inc 1, PM, work Lace Pattern as set to last st, k1.

Row 2: K to marker, RM, inc 1, PM, k to end (2 sts increased on one ridge).

Double Increase Ridge

Row 1: Inc 1, work Lace Pattern as set to marker, RM, inc 1, PM, work Lace Pattern as set to last st, k1.

Row 2: Inc 1, k to marker, RM, inc 1, PM, k to end (4 sts increased on ridge).

Even Ridge

Row 1: K1, work Lace Pattern as set to marker, RM, inc 1, PM, work Lace Pattern to last 2 sts, k2tog.

Row 2: K to marker, RM, inc 1, PM, k to last 2 sts, k2tog.

Decrease Ridge

Row 1: K1, work Lace Pattern to marker, RM, inc 1, PM, work Lace Pattern to last 4 sts, k2tog, k2tog.

Row 2: K to marker, RM, inc 1, PM, k to last 4 sts, k2tog, k2tog (2 sts decreased on ridge).

To work sleeve cap, alternate Single Increase Ridge and Double Increase Ridge 8 (9, 9, 10) (10, 11) times—66 (72, 72, 78) (78, 84) sts. Then work Double Increase Ridge 0 (0, 1, 0) (1, 1) time. Then work Single Increase Ridge 0 (0, 0, 1) (0, 0) time— 66 (72, 76, 80) (82, 88) sts.

Sleeve cap is completed.

Sleeve length

Shape sleeve length as follows:

Work (1 Even Ridge, followed by 1 Decrease Ridge) 2 (2, 4, 6)(5, 14) times. Then work (2 Even Ridges, followed by 1 Decrease Ridge) 1 (8, 8, 7)(8, 2) times. Then work (3 Even Ridges, followed by 1 Decrease Ridge) 6 (1, 0, 0)(0, 0) times—48 (50, 52, 54)(56, 56) sts remain.

Squaring off cuff edge

Work each side separately. Keeping first half of sts (with working yarn attached) on needle, place remaining half of sts on a holder.

Row 1: K2tog, work Lace Pattern as set to end, turn; SKP, k to last 2 sts, p2tog, turn.

Repeat Row 1 until 3 sts remain, then k3, turn; SKP, p1. Bind off remaining 2 sts.

Cut yarn.

Transfer sts from holder back to needle. Attach yarn at top to continue working second side as follows:

Row 1: SKP, k to last 2 sts, p2tog, turn; k1, work Lace Pattern as set to end, turn.

Repeat Row 1 until 3 sts remain, then SKP, bind off remaining st. Cut yarn.

FINISHING

Block all pieces to measurements. With right sides of front and back together, sew shoulder and side seams, using tapestry needle threaded with yarn to work backstitch.

Sew underarm seams of sleeves. Sew a sleeve to each armhole, matching center top of cap to shoulder seams and sleeve seam to side seam.

Crocheted edging

With crochet hook work a row of single crochet (sc) around neckline and bottom edge of sweater.

This project was knit with 4 (4, 5, 5,)(6, 6) skeins of Artyarns Silk Rhapsody, 100% silk and 70% mohair/30% silk blend medium-weight 2-strand yarn, 3½oz/100g = 260yd/238m per skein, color #143, variegated browns and blues.

BONUS PROJECT

WANT MORE USING THIS TECHNIQUE?
VISIT WWW.ARTYARNS.COM

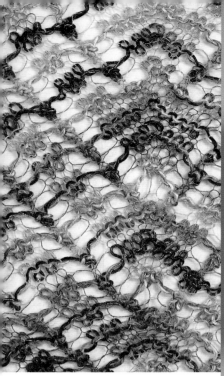

Celestial Tie Wrap Jacket

■

EXPERIENCE LEVEL

SIZE
One size fits most (Small to Large).

T HE CROSS-OVER DESIGN OF
THIS WRAP EMPHASIZES THE
BUSTLINE WHILE VISUALLY
CINCHING THE WAIST TO
HOURGLASS PROPORTIONS.
SUBTLE METALLIC THREADS
WINK LIKE EVENING STARS
WHEN CAUGHT BY LIGHT.

FINISHED MEASUREMENTS

Bust: About 35"/89cm, measured flat and unstretched. Garment stretches to at least 42"/107cm at bust.

MATERIALS

Approx total: 520y/476m silk and mohair/silk blend with metallic medium-weight 3-strand yarn (yarn A), and

230yd/210m mohair/silk blend superfine yarn (yarn B)

Circular needles: 5mm (size 8 U.S.) *or size to obtain gauge*, at 24"/61cm long

Crochet hook: 3.25mm (size D/3 U.S.) for finishing

Stitch marker

3 stitch holders

Tapestry needle for finishing

GAUGE

12 sts and 16 rows = 4"/10cm in Pattern Stitch

Always take time to check your gauge.

PATTERN STITCH

LP: yo, sl1, k2tog, psso, yo

INSTRUCTIONS

JACKET

Note: This jacket is made in 6 steps: the right front lower triangle, right front arm-edge section, the back section, right sleeve that also joins back to right front, left front, and left sleeve that also joins the back to the left front. The directions will guide you through the process.

Pattern Notes: As in the Filigree Wrap (page 130), Lace Panels are established in the first 16 rows. Continue to work Lace Panels as set, checking your knitting to make sure each LP lines up over the one from the previous pattern row. Add new Lace Panels as needed whenever there are 6 knit sts between the last LP and the edge or center sts. When decreasing in pattern, discontinue working a Lace Panel when there are not enough sts to work the full 3-stitch pattern, and knit these sts instead. There should always be 3 knit sts between Lace Panels.

STEP 1: RIGHT FRONT TRIANGLE WITH CENTER INCREASES

Starting with yarn A, cast on 3 sts. Work back and forth in rows on circular needles throughout.

Work Rows 1 to 20 of Filigree Wrap on page 132, alternating A and B in the following sequence—Rows 1 to 4: work with A, Rows 5–6: B, Rows 7–8: A, Rows 9–10: B, rows 11–12: A, Rows 13–14: B, Rows 15–16: A, Rows 17–18: B, Rows 19–20: A.

Rows 21 through 35: Repeat Rows 19 and 20, alternating B and A every 2 rows as before, and remembering to insert new Lace Panels as needed whenever there are 6 knit sts together; work until there are 72 sts, ending with a RS row.

STEP 2: RIGHT FRONT ARM-EDGE SECTION

Without turning work, slide sts to opposite end of needle, with sts again at left-hand tip of needle ready to be worked again. With B, bind off 36 sts. Return remaining 36 sts to other end of needle, and with A, k to end (at upper point of triangle).

Continue on these 36 sts as follows:

Row 1 (RS): With B, k3, work LP as set to last 2 sts, p2tog.

Row 2: With B, k to end.

Row 3: With A, k1, work LP as established to last 2 sts, p2tog.

Row 4: With A, k to end.

Rows 5 through 36: Repeat Rows 3 and 4, alternating yarns B and A, until 18 sts remain, ending with a wrong-side row in A.

With A, working on the wrong side of work and using Knitted Cast-on Method (see page 20), cast on 18 additional sts. Place all 36 sts on a stitch holder. Cut A and B.

STEP 3: BACK

Repeat Step 1 to make lower triangle—72 sts.

Continue to alternate yarns every 2 rows as before, squaring off the arm-edges as follows:

Row 1 (RS): With B, k1, work LP as established to marker, RM, inc 1, PM, work LP as established to last 2 sts, p2tog.

Row 2: With B, k to marker, RM, inc 1, PM, k to last 2 sts, p2tog. Change yarns.

Rows 3 through 36: Repeat Rows 1 and 2, ending with a WS row worked with A. Place half (36) of the sts on one stitch holder and the remaining 36 sts on another holder.

STEP 4: RIGHT SLEEVE, JOINING BACK AND RIGHT FRONT

With right side of back facing you, starting at the bottommost side of the triangle, transfer the 36 sts of the right half of the back onto the circular needle with the triangle top at the top of the needle; then loading sts from the left, still with right side of work facing you, add the sts from the right front holder, starting with the 18 cast-on sts, then the 18 worked sts—72 sts in all with the bottommost st of the back at the needle tip, ready to be worked. Attach B.

Row 1 (RS): With B, work LP as set to last st of cast-on group, k2tog (combining last back st to first

cast-on st), PM, work LP to last st, p1.

Row 2: With B, k to marker, RM, k2tog, PM, k to last st, p1. Change yarns.

Row 3: With A, work LP as set to marker, RM, k2tog, PM, work LP to last st, p1.

Row 4: With A, k to marker, RM, k2tog, PM, k to last st, p1.

Row 5: With B, inc 1, work LP as set to marker, RM, k2 tog, PM, work LP to last st, p1.

Row 6: With B, inc 1, k to marker, RM, k2tog, k to last st, p1.

Repeat Rows 3 through 6 until sleeve measures 22"/56cm from underarm.

Sleeve cuff

Continuing on remaining sleeve sts, work as follows:

Row 1: K1, work LP to marker, RM, k2tog, PM, work LP as set to last 2 sts, p2tog.

Row 2: K1, k to marker, RM, k2tog, PM, k to last 2 sts, p2tog.

Repeat Rows 1 and 2 until 4 are left.

Next row: K1, k2tog, k1.

Following Row: Sl 1, k2tog, psso. Cut yarn; weave in ends.

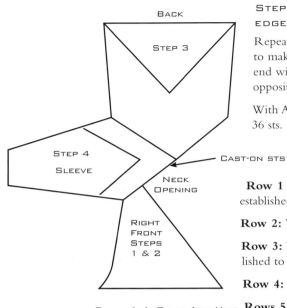

BACK

STEP 3

STEP 4

SLEEVE

CAST-ON STS

NECK OPENING

RIGHT FRONT STEPS 1 & 2

STEPS 1-4: RIGHT ARM UNIT

STEP 5: LEFT FRONT ARM-EDGE SECTION

Repeat Rows 1 through 35 of Step 1 to make triangle for left front. You will end with A at one side and B at opposite side of piece.

With A, bind off 36 sts, k remaining 36 sts.

Work on these 36 sts as follows:

Row 1 (RS): With B, k1, work LP as established to last st, k1.

Row 2: With B, k to last 2 sts, p2tog.

Row 3: With A, k1, work LP as established to last st, k1.

Row 4: With A, k to last 2 sts, p2tog.

Rows 5 through 36: Repeat Rows 1 through 4, alternating yarns B and A every 2 rows until 18 sts remain, ending with a wrong-side row in A.

Cut yarns.

With wrong side of work still facing you, slide stitches to other end of needle. Attach A and using Knitted Cast On (page 20), cast on 18 more sts. Cut A. Place all 36 sts on a holder.

STEP 6: LEFT SLEEVE, JOINING BACK AND LEFT FRONT

Holding back with right side of work facing you, starting at bottommost side of triangle, transfer the 36 sts of the remaining half of back to needle with triangle top stitch at top of needle. Slide sts to center of needle. Working from the right, add sts from Left Front holder, starting with the 18 cast-on sts, followed by the 18 worked sts, sliding them to the right to meet the back sts—72 sts in all; the first st at the needle point is the bottommost st of the left front, ready to be worked. Attach B.

Row 1 (RS): With B, work LP as set to last cast-on st of left front, k2tog (combining last

---

cast-on st front and first st of back, PM, work LP as set to last st, p1.

Row 2: With B, k to marker, RM, k2tog, PM, k to last st, p1.

Row 3: With A, work LP as set to marker, RM, k2tog, PM, work LP as set to last st, p1.

Row 4: With A, k to marker, RM, k2tog, PM, k to last st, p1.

Row 5: With B, inc 1, work LP as set to marker, RM, k2 tog, PM, work LP as set to last st, p1.

Row 6: With B, inc 1, k to marker, RM, k2tog, k to last st, p1.

Repeat Rows 3 through 6 until sleeve measures 22"/56cm from underarm.

Sleeve cuff

Work same as right sleeve.

FINISHING

With wrong side facing, starting at bottom and working to underarm, sew front to back at right side seam, then continue seaming right sleeve. Repeat on left side.

Crocheted ties

Attach yarn A to bottom corner of left front, and with crochet hook, *chain 2, sc in last chain st; rep from * until cord measures 32"/82cm. Cut yarn, and weave in ends with tapestry needle.

In same manner, make a 12"/30.5cm cord on right front.

Weave in all ends.

This project was knit with 2 skeins of Artyarns Silk Rhapsody Glitter, 100% silk and 70% mohair/30% silk blend with 100% Lurex metallic strand medium-weight 3-strand yarn, 3½ oz/100g = 260yd/238m per skein, color #148S, variegated gray/black with silver metallic (yarn A), and

1 skein of Artyarns Silk Mohair, 70% kid mohair/30% silk blend superfine yarn, .9oz/25g = 230yd/210m per skein, color #148, variegated gray/black (yarn B).

BACK

CAST-ON STS

NECK OPENING

RIGHT FRONT

SLEEVE STEP 6

LEFT FRONT

STEP 5

STEPS 5-6: LEFT ARM UNIT

ACKNOWLEDGMENTS

There are many people who made this book possible, and I am so grateful to them all.

Thanks to the Westchester Knitting Guild and Nanette, who helped me round up volunteer knitters to finish everything in this book in a timely manner. Patty and Dorothy, this book would not have been completed on time without your knitting and design assistance—thank you wholeheartedly. Judi, your support was so important to me. Robin, Marcia, Ann, Olive, Jane, your help on projects, and knitting (and sometimes re-knitting) is incredibly appreciated. Marcia and Ann, thank you for letting me use your daughters as models. And thanks to the amazingly supportive Yahoo Multidirectional Group and to volunteer testers like Lindsay, Vickie, Terri, Kelly, etc…

Shirley, my teacher, you are an inspiration to me. Your design classes opened my eyes to the possibilities. Cynthia, thank you for letting me teach the Diagonal Sweater Workshop at your beautiful shop, Knitting Central. Laurie, I enjoyed teaching the Tamarah Shawl at your amazing store, Sticks and Strings, and once again it helped me create the tutorial for following your lace.

Jim and Terry at Colonial Needle, thank you for supplying me with the wonderful needles that I used to create these pieces. Your rosewood needles are unsurpassed. Fanny, bless you for being such a good knitter, and helping me with projects for this book.

Ellen, thank you for tech editing the book and helping me improve the patterns. Linda, oh Linda…what can I say! It was a real pleasure to work with a professional editor like you and so incredibly helpful. Dana, you have outdone yourself with the photography. And thank you to Lark, my publisher—Carol and Nicole, I appreciate your support and your belief in me.

And the gals at Artyarns: Simone, Mariella, and Arali, and others who made sure the yarns were prepared to my specifications, thank you.

Last but not least, I want to thank my husband Elliot, who once again stood by me, preparing dinner and helping with the kids as I barricaded myself in a room to complete the book's deadlines. Ruth, you were incredibly helpful with last-minute knitting, while Rita enthusiastically gave words of encouragement. And Owen and Jason, I appreciate that you never once complained.

YARN SUBSTITUTION CHART

Near the beginning of each project in this book, you'll find the weight, material, and color of each yarn in the piece shown. At the end of the project, you'll find the number of the specific yarns from Artyarns, Inc. (www.artyarns.com) that were used. The following chart provides a number of yarn varieties from other manufacturers that are the equivalent weight and composition of those from Artyarns.

Yarn in Project	Weight	Substitute Yarns
Artyarns Cashmere 2	**2** FINE	**Monarch** by Alchemy **Cashmere** by Bernat **Peruvian Baby Cashmere** by Elann **Mongolian Cashmere** by Jade Sapphire **Light-Weight Cashmere** by Karabella **Supercashmere Fine** by Karabella **Seta/Cashmere** by Lana Grossa **Classic Cashcotton 4 Ply** by Rowan **Classic Cashsoft 4 Ply** by Rowan **Cachemir Anny** by Anny Blatt
Artyarns Regal Silk	**2** FINE	**Pure Silk** by Debbie Bliss **Silk Purse** by Alchemy **Luxury** by Filatura di Crosa **Shangri La** by Bouton d'Or **Silky Wool** by Elsebeth Lavoid **Tao** by Colinette **La Luz** by Fiesta **Pure & Simple** by Tilli Thomas **Tussah Silk** by Tess **Amerah** by South West Trading Company
Artyarns Silk Ribbon	**2** FINE	Any Artyarns Regal Silk (or substitute)
Artyarns Silk Mohair	**1** SUPER FINE	**Kid Mohair** by Adriafil **Kidsilk Haze** by Rowan **Extra Fine Mohair** by Be Sweet **Kid Seta** by Madil **Douceur et Soie** by K1C2 Any **Silk Mohair A** by Habu **Mohair Luxe** by Lang **Parisienne** by Colinette **Super Kydd** by Elann **Baby Kid Extra** by Filatura Di Crosa
Artyarns Supermerino	**4** MEDIUM	**220 Wool** by Cascade **Classic Merino Wool** by Patons **Kureyon** by Noro **Sugar'n Cream** by Lily **Lamb's Pride Worsted** by Brown Sheep **Meriono Worsted** by Malabrigo **Simply Soft** by Caron **Silk Garden** by Noro **Shepherd Worsted** by Loran's Laces **Merino** by Lana Grossa

continued on page 144

continued from page 143

Yarn in Project	Weight	Substitute Yarns
Artyarns Ultramerino 4	**2** FINE	**Koigu Painter's Palette Premium Merino (KPPPM)** by Koigu **Shepherd Sock** by Lorna's Laces **Zarina** by Filatura di Crosa **Sassy Stripes** by Cascade **Socks that Rock** by Blue Moon Fiber Arts **Basic Merino Socks** by Fleece Artist **Supersock** by Cherry Tree Hill **Soxie** by Great Adirondack **Saki** by Prism Any **Trekking** by Zitron
Artyarns Ultramerino 8	**4** MEDIUM	**220 Wool** by Cascade **Classic Merino Wool** by Patons **Kureyon** by Noro **Simply Soft** by Caron **Silk Garden** by Noro **Sugar'n Cream** by Lily **Lamb's Pride Worsted** by Brown Sheep **Meriono Worsted** by Malabrigo **Aurora 8** by Karabella **Handspun Wool** by Manos Del Uruguay
Artyarns Silk Rhapsody	**4** MEDIUM	Hold any Artyarns Silk Mohair (or substitute) with a strand of Artyarns Regal Silk

ABOUT THE AUTHOR

Iris Schreier is the author of *Reversible Knits* (Lark, 2009), *Lacy Little Knits* (Lark, 2007) and is the co-author of *Exquisite Little Knits* (Lark, 2004). Her original and innovative techniques are being used in knitting workshops and design schools around the world, and her patterns have been translated into multiple languages. Iris has appeared on various television shows and has written articles and published patterns for leading

knitting magazines. She founded Artyarns to produce yarns and color combinations for her designs that were not available commercially. The company's world-renowned line of yarns now encompasses unusual and intriguing combinations of fibers—some with embellishments—that are all hand-painted in luscious colorways to work optimally with her patterns. To view more of Iris's designs and yarns and watch videos of her techniques, visit www.irisknits.com. Iris lives and works in White Plains, New York.